ILARIA CABULA - гклі.

Criminology and Criminal Profiling for beginners

(crime scene forensics, serial killers and sects)

Preface

By Arnaldo Lovecchio

It is with great pleasure that I write these few lines of introduction to this work. A pleasure that derives from the deep interest that I have for criminology, which I have been studying for some time. Nowadays we hear very often about criminology, serial killers and heinous murders. We hear about them on the news, cinema, literature, video games; the serial murderer has now polarized a good part of the media expression. Who has never heard of Dr. Hannibal Lecter, or Dexter Morgan? And who has never seen an episode of CSI? But how much truth is there in what we see? How do serial killers act? How do they choose their victims? And why do they kill? Do investigation techniques really work as we see in TV shows? These questions find their answers in this book, perfect for anyone who wants to approach the study of this discipline. The first six chapters deal with the origins of criminology, the analysis of the different categories of serial killers and the numerous investigation techniques used during the crime scene analysis. The remaining four chapters focus on the analysis of the phenomenon of satanic sects: here we study the mental manipulation techniques used by sects; also, we'll study their victims and their influence on society and young people.

Good reading!

GENERAL INDEX

Readings strictly recommended in the volume and bibliography.

666- the Ghost Book.

Chapter One

"Was criminology born in Europe?"

"Now and then, alas, the conscience of man takes up
a burden so heavy in horror that it can be
thrown down only into the grave.
And thus the essence of all crime is undivulged."

EDGAR ALLAN POE

To answer this question we need to investigate the historical basis of the profession and take, without further delay, a wonderful journey that will lead us to the present day. To explain how to become a criminologist, it is appropriate to deal with a short story on the origin, history and evolution of this fascinating discipline. The very first dawn of criminology can in fact be traced back to the European Enlightenment. Many authors claim that criminology was born in the eighteenth century with the treatise of the Italian jurist Cesare Beccaria: *"On crimes and punishments"*. From the premise of the treaty we can read: *"he laws, which although they are or ought to be pacts of free men, were for the most part only the instruments of the passions of some few, or born from a fortuitous and passing necessity; not already dictated by a cold examiner of human nature, who in one place concentrated the actions of a multitude of men, and considered them from this point of view: maximum happiness divided into the greatest number"*. The punishments, according to said author, are therefore aimed both at preventing the perpetrator from breaking the laws again, and at diverting other citizens from committing similar faults. The punishments must therefore be chosen in proportion to the crime committed and must be able to leave an indelible impression on men, without however being excessively tormenting or unnecessarily severe for those who have violated the law. During the mid-nineteenth century, criminology rose to the rank of autonomous science. Also in these years, Cesare Lombroso published *"The Delinquent Man"*.

Lombroso is considered the father and founder of criminal science, since he's the one who introduced the basis for the crime analysis methodologies. Referring to the European doctrines of innate and biologically conditioned crime, Lombroso argues that the atypical conduct of the delinquent or genius is conditioned, as well as by social and economic environmental components, by factors independent of the will; ponderous factors, such as heredity and nervous diseases, which decrease the responsibility of the criminal, since he is primarily a patient. In particular, in the work *"The delinquent man"* Lombroso maintains the bold thesis according to which: *"(...) criminal behavior is determined by physiological predispositions, which often reveal themselves also externally in the anatomical configuration of the skull"* Lombroso's thought can be summed up in one of his famous phrases: *"... the criminal is an atavistic being who reproduces on his own person the fierce instincts of primitive humanity and lower animals"*. Genius and madness were two elements that Lombroso associated.

At the beginning, Lombroso had to fight to eradicate the ethical-moral prejudices relating to delinquency, which were deeply rooted in the social substratum. In fact, most of his contemporary scholars continued to consider delinquents solely guilty, considering Lombroso's studies irrelevant. Despite this, the theory of the epileptic equivalence of the crime (or rather, of its epileptic component) gained ground, although proclaimed relatively late, but already identifiable in texts such as *Genius and Folly* and *Du démon de Socrate*, by Lélut (1836). The interest in genius also stemmed from residual Enlightenment-related conceptions of an image of history as "catastrophic" (in the Greek sense of catastrophè), characterized by sudden upheavals caused by natural or individual causes, that is, genes. Theory endorsed by emerging evolutionism contemporary to Lombroso, which tended to consider geniuses as a certain subspecies of heroes. In a publication by Lombroso on the subject, *"On the diseases of men given to intellectual works"*, the link between genius and madness was conceived, which had connected to these two factors also physical peculiarities, found by Lombroso in madmen. In the various asylums in which he conducted his analysis Lombroso, in addition to finding the defects and the individual anomalies, had also discovered flashes of genius and passion, cultivating hypotheses that in some ways distanced him from epileptic theory. He had been very impressed by the ideas of the madmen, by their ingenious works and their prodigious calculations, continuing on the road according to which among the madmen the founders of religions and parties such as, for example, Luther, Savonarola and Joan of Arc, abound. The distractions of the geniuses were considered by Lombroso as moments of epileptic absence, as well as their nocturnal visions (in Dostoevsky, Maupassant, Musset), melancholies (Voltaire, Molière, Chopin, Giusti), suicide attempts (Rousseau, Cavour, Chateaubriand), the megalomanias (Muhammad, Colombo, Savonarola, Bruno), shyness (Leopardi), infant love (Dante, Alfieri, Byron). Physically speaking, Lombroso asserted the predominance among the geniuses of characteristics such as: pallor, thinness or obesity, being rickety, sterile or unmarried, brains for the most part of greater than average volume and with deformities, such as the abnormal sutures in the skull of Alessandro Volta. Then there were also cases in which the geniuses were totally and irreversibly crazy, and not only in some moments or in latent manifestations, like Tasso, Gogol, Ampère, Kant and Beethoven. However, together with these character analysis, Lombroso also supported some more questionable theories, such as that that large barometric variations and a strong heat would affect madness, great discoveries or more acute observations (citing Malpighi's cases as examples and Galvani). From 1876 he disseminated his anthropological theory of delinquency in the five subsequent editions of *The Delinquent Man*, which subsequently expanded into a multi-volume work. Being among the greatest physiognomics scholars of that time, Lombroso measured the shape and size of the skulls of many brigands killed and brought from the South of Italy to Piedmont, drawing the conclusion that the ancestral traits that they presented dated back to primitive man. Indeed what he developed was a new pseudoscience dealing with forensic phrenology. He deduced that criminals carried anti-social traits from birth, by inheritance, which today is considered completely unfounded. Note that Lombroso had developed the theory of atavism a year before the publication of *"On the origin of species"*, by Charles Darwin (1859). In fact, his work in the first half of the twentieth century was instrumentalized in the context of eugenics and by certain forms of *"scientific racism"*. Lombroso always strongly supported the need for capital punishment within the Italian legal system. In fact, he believed that if the criminal was such for his physical conformation, no form of rehabilitation was possible, thus identifying the objective to which the criminal system had to aim for the security of society. Some of the strangest and most particular studies carried out by Lombroso during his research life were: *The wrinkle of the idiot and the anomaly of the scalp, The origin of the kiss, Why the priests dress as women.* In 1891 he published, in collaboration with Filippo Cougnet, a book entitled *"Studies on the professional signs of porters"* and, in 1896, a work on epileptic Dante. An important "involuntary" collaborator of Lombroso was Giuseppe Villella, born in Motta di Santa Lucia (Cosenza) and presumably died in Pavia, convicted for arson and theft and suspected of brigandage. It was from the autopsy of his corpse that Lombroso discovered the so-called "median occipital fossa": the anomaly of the cranial structure responsible, he said, for deviant behaviors of the "criminal type".

The remains of Lombroso are also preserved in the Museum of criminal anthropology, in the so-called called "Lombroso Collection" at the Institute of forensic medicine in Turin. By his last will, his entire skeleton is preserved in a display case, and the skull-free head in formalin. In a recent anthropometry study, *"The true story of Pulcinella's skull"*, the Neapolitan naturalist Dario David highlighted that in a fairly large sample of individuals, consisting of ex-prisoners, compared with a sample of individuals never subjected to prison measures , the somatic traits of the "delinquent" of Lombroso had significantly different percentages depending on the district of Naples from which the sample came; 50% in some popular areas (Forcella, Sanità, Quartieri Spagnoli and especially Cavone), 12% in all other districts. The most probable cause, being the samples from different areas of the same city, seems to be the fact that those somatic features developed abundantly in particularly closed and isolated areas (socially and geographically), where the crystallization of a given character is easier. In these same areas there was a regime of poverty and abandonment for over 400 years and therefore there was a greater risk of criminal outbreak (compared to other neighborhoods in the same city).

In a certain sense, we can now speak of "Lombroso's reasons": the concomitance between somatic traits and human behavior could exist, but certainly not according to the direct cause-effect link of the atavistic theory, which was hypothesized by the author. From a methodological and statistical point of view, Lombroso's texts are incomplete due to the smallness and lack of balance of the samples considered, and this further damages the scientific nature of the conclusions obtained. The idea that crime is connected to certain physical characteristics of a person is very ancient: it is already found, for example, in Homer's Iliad, in whose book II the deviance of Thersites is directly linked to his physical ugliness. The laws of the European Middle Ages stipulated that if two people had been suspected of a crime, the more deformed of the two would have been considered guilty. In the nineteenth century, with the birth of the empirical sciences - sociology and criminal anthropology - a new cultural current spread, the positive school, which focused on two different thematic areas.

From here on, we will find ourselves facing a first dichotomous polarization regarding the scientific approach to matter:

- scientific approach (biological - medical - psychiatric): in addition to the aforementioned positive method, it can be traced back to the new science of the human being: psychology, thanks to the founding fathers of those times, G. Jung and S. Freud.

- forensic approach (sociological - anthropological - juridical): given by the different criminological subjects. First of all, law, supported by disciplines such as statistics, sociology of law and anthropology itself; these disciplines paint the social framework in which the individual moves, more or less stimulated to become guilty in relation to the class of belonging.

These two strands, psychological and sociological, still persist and those who want to pursue the profession of criminologist must take this into account. In addition, to date, we can observe how brilliant criminologists come from university studies in Communication Sciences, Educational Sciences, Nursing Sciences. Criminology is an empirical and inductive science that analyzes and studies the criminal phenomenon in its complexity: crimes, victims, perpetrators, crime perception, preventive techniques. The good criminologist "gets his hands dirty", experiments, closes himself in the alchemist's laboratory and remains there until he has turned the lead of the clues into the gold of the evidence. All this through real scientific research on the causal links of crime. It is therefore an interdisciplinary and syncretic path that embraces various areas such as: psychology, law, anthropology, biology, statistics, medicine, a sort of "big bang" between the humanities and the legal sciences. All expressions of the same unitary representation: crime, understood as any fact having legal relevance, under the aspect of criminal law. The term criminology today does not comprehensively encompass the topic because over time it has taken on various nuances that would each deserve a specific denomination. Secondly, precisely because of the need for a scientific evaluation of crime, criminalistics has developed; this discipline studies the application of sciences, such as chemistry, physics, ballistics, biology, entomology, forensic archeology. Criminalistics is a minefield, full of pitfalls. It is very easy to think of having found a correspondence between two bullets, even if it is purely apparent; it is very easy to think that you have found gunshot residues, while instead you simply have normal dust in front of you; it is very easy to think that we have found the identity between fingerprints or between traces of DNA, while instead we have only tried to make the results match what we hope to find. Focusing on the phenomenology of crimes (murder, rape, organized crime, terrorism, domestic violence, etc.), criminology has the task of "classifying" the various types of offenders; imputable and otherwise, habitual, by trend, professional etc. However, one must always take into consideration the motive and emotional state of the subject, his capacity to understand and want, therefore studying his mental abilities, as well as drug addiction or alcohol addiction.

We recall here that under Italian law, if the culprit lacks this ability, he would not be imputable. Recent statistics have shown that the criminal instinct is more common among men, even ten times higher than that of women, and the "accused" age group is between 20 and 35 years old. The approach to the study of crime can be of a micro or macroscopic type: in the first case, an attempt is made to understand the "spark" of the crime, assessing the personality of the individual criminal, his tendency to commit a crime and his defects in socialization. In the second case, an attempt is made to understand general crime trends, in order to contribute to the development of law enforcement policies. Criminology is also envisaged as a complementary teaching subject in the degree courses in law, psychology, legal sciences, defense and security sciences. Some subjects of study on the subject of criminology are: criminological theories and techniques, activity and role of the criminologist, criminal profiling, analysis of the crime scene, criminological interview, criminological expertise, stalking, sexual crimes and pedophilia, serial killers, mass murderers, drugs and drug addictions, penitentiary system. Here's a list of the principles that regulate this matter and that we will apply in the rest of the volume.

1. the correct answer is usually the most logical one (the so-called logical principle or Occam's razor);

2. the observed phenomenon must be reproducible, according to technical profiles (the so-called scientific principle);

3. the observer of the phenomenon must be free from psychological and psychiatric conditions, so as not to compromise the judgment (the so-called socio-psycho-pedagogical principle);

4. the event must be the result of a precise conduct, logically and causally connected to the action or omission put in place (the so-called legal or conditional principle or condicio sine qua non);

5. the event must be the result of an action or omission by a "tangible" entity, therefore a presence that possesses a physical body or that can interact with the physical and chemical forces causing a shift (the so-called chemical - physical principle or materialistic principle);

6. the event carried out must leave significant consequences in the group to which the passive subject belongs (the so-called anthropological principle);

7. the phenomenon must be explained using the typical analytical method of the investigation (the so-called investigative principle).

In any case, to carry out the profession of criminologist you must have an encyclopedic culture and you must necessarily have high deductive skills, devote yourself to humility and be animated by a constant desire for knowledge.

Special content: Sherlock Holmes, the first criminologist

Sherlock Holmes, a character born from the superb pen of the Scottish writer Sir Arthur Ignatius Conan Doyle, was the first detective in the history of fiction. In the first story *"A Study in Scarlet"* Sir Conan Doyle puts his criminal skills into practice. It must be said that Doyle was a doctor and, perhaps, this is why his character is so skilled in solving any investigation. Sherlock Holmes, in addition to being very deductive, has knowledge of botany, anatomy, geology, chemistry, fencing, boxing, sensational literature and law. As described in *"A Study in Scarlet"* the historic meeting between Watson and Holmes takes place in 1881, in the chemistry laboratory of St Bartholomew's Hospital, in London : *"a large attic room where a myriad of bottles lined up"*. On that occasion, as the young and brilliant criminologist Beatrice Pecora tells in her writings, Holmes first meets Dr. John Watson, who will then become his helper. The detective shows his assistant a new discovery related to the recognition of blood, thus making his first professional gesture as a true criminalist!

"Let us have some fresh blood", *he said, digging a long bodkin into his finger, and drawing off the resulting drop of blood in a*

chemical pipette. "Now, I add this small quantity of blood to a liter of water. You perceive that the resulting mixture has the appearance of pure water. The proportion of blood cannot be more than one in a million. I have no doubt, however, that we shall be able to obtain the characteristic reaction". As he spoke, he threw into the vessel a few white crystals, and then added some drops of a transparent fluid. In an instant the contents assumed a dull mahogany color, and a brownish dust was precipitated to the bottom of the glass jar".

Scientists wondered if this test was just a literary fiction of Conan Doyle or if it was scientifically founded. To answer this question we must take a step back. Before 1875 there was a microscopic examination of red blood cells that distinguished between mammals and non-mammals, from the hematin test and the ammonia test. In addition, Holmes also cites the test of the guaiac or better known as occult blood. It consists of a hydroalcoholic solution of vegetable resin, to which a small amount of the presumed blood and hydrogen peroxide is added. If the material is blood, a blue color appears. Most blood tests are based on the same principle: peroxidase, a large family of blood enzymes that act as a catalyst thanks to the oxidation of a chemical compound, such as acetic acid or propionic acid, which produces a characteristic color. The clear crystals could be oxidants such as peroxide or sodium perborate. In no other story Sherlock speaks of chemical tests: more than anything else he adheres to giving solutions on court cases thanks to his intuition and good observation of the crime scene. Thus, Mr. Holmes will become an investigator rather than an expert in forensic chemistry.

Post Scriptum: in the novels that tell the deeds of Sherlock Holmes there is no trace of the phrase *"Elementary, Watson!"*. This famous expression appears only on one page of the collection: *"The memoirs of Sherlock Holmes"* and, more precisely in the story: *"The Adventure of the Crooked Man"*. Holmes, answering a question by Watson, pronounces the term: *"Elementary!"*.

Expression that he uses just twice in the story *"A Study in Scarlet"*.

Chapter Two
"Murder and criminology"

"One murder makes a villain, millions a hero.

Numbers sanctify."

SIR CHARLES CHAPLIN

When investigating a murder case, you must have at least one of the following to find the culprit:

1. a (spontaneous) confession;

2. a witness (direct/de relato);

3. a material proof (depending on the categories of law).

To identify witnesses and evidence, investigators follow a path that includes the study of the characteristics of the perpetrator (criminal profiling), the victim (victimology) and the analysis of the crime scene. Particular attention must be paid to the study of the victims, who can provide a lot of useful information to understand the murderer's psychology. The majority of the murders are committed due to a motive that we can define as "trivial" (jealousy, revenge, economic interest). In these cases, the motive leaps "immediately to the eye" of the investigator and directs him in the investigation towards a suspect who has some kind of relationship with the victim. Instead, in a serial murder case, we are faced with a type of motivation internal to the subject that kills, a psychological pleasure that, at least in the first phase, does not translate into evident material traces to be "found" on the crime scene.

In this hypothesis, a particular type of investigation must be faced, which presents specific problems and in which the use of particular investigation techniques is necessary. In order to screen the investigations in the right direction, a careful analysis of the crime scene must be carried out through the so-called site inspection. In this activity, it may be useful to have photographic reproduction techniques using analog or digital media, to document every detail of the crime scene. In Italy, for example, the crime scene is analyzed and studied through the use of "expert protocols" such as the Automatic System for Technical Surveys (SART) or by resorting to stereoscopic photogrammetry techniques. All this by storing the entire multimedia documentation in the Central Information System of the Scientific Police, which allows the digital archiving of the images and a comparison of the same according to some primary research keys. Other investigation techniques indispensable for solving cases of this type are the "psychological profile" and the "geographical profile". The investigator can field as many moves as his imagination, professional ability and experience suggest.

The choice of times for each strategic phase will be of fundamental importance for the investigator (work slot and activity timing). The good investigator will also have to pay attention to the analysis of the news, the importance and weighting of the archives, the "*open*" and confidential sources of information, information and counter-information, on blogs and the Internet. Sometimes even a "forgotten on the street" garbage bag can allow investigators to solve a case. Without generalizing, we can say that: "*the investigation of the murders puts Italian police forces in difficulty to the point that some criminologists claim that in Italy the murder pays, in the sense that seven times out of ten the perpetrator is not identified by investigators*". By taking a look at the serial killings instead, the US police forces have proven to be particularly skilled and effective in identifying the various serial killers who have so far appeared in the limelight. In the serial repetition of the murder, the author still makes (consciously?) mistakes that lead investigators to his identification sooner or later. The problems emerge more not with serial killers but with isolated cases, that is, with the murderers of a single crime. To reconstruct the crime from its design to the author's exit from the crime scene, it is essential to start from the data that can be collected by carrying out an inspection on the scene. The crime scene must be kept "*frozen*" for as long as possible and "*aseptic*" from contamination by various visitors (policemen, technicians, journalists, technical consultants). From the crime scene, it is necessary to collect all the biological evidence belonging to both the victim and the attacker, also identifying them with the help of ultraviolet rays and similar devices used by the crime scene investigators. It is then necessary to triangulate this information with that collected from any deposition, as well as with the data detectable by the autopsy. From the response of the corpse, the coroner will be able to clarify the type, sequence and nature of the injuries that have been inflicted on the victim and thus establish the cause and modalities of the death.

The coroner will be able to establish a fundamental element: whether death was an accidental event or a desired event, and how it happened. Based on all the findings on the inspection and other autopsy evidence, it is therefore possible to reconstruct the interaction between the murderer and the victim at the crime scene, and therefore the dynamics of the murder. Once the dynamics of what (probably) happened at the crime scene are known, it is possible to identify the possible motive. If identifying the motive is not possible, it is important to establish that the murder is "devoid of an apparent motive" thus triggering the investigation path of the murder on a psychopathological basis (most of the time pertaining to a serial killer). The author "sees" the whole scene over and over again in his mind, like in a movie, and associates it with fantastic thoughts and emotions. The serial killer imagines the facts over and over again: he sees the perfect, fulfilling, rewarding, desirable scene. In the end, he elaborates the crime as an inevitable, necessary, indifferent act. It will be the gratifications of these thoughts and the pleasure of these emotions that oblige him to continue in the conception and planning of the crime until its realization. Having seen and revised the scene several times in his mind, at the time of the crime the killer does not improvise, but puts in place a sequence of acts "already lived, already acted" and this makes him appear even more brutal, determined, bad, the "monster" which will then appear in the newspapers. After having reconstructed the maturation of the murderous project in the mind of the author, in a state of lucidity or madness, the investigator poses the problem of reconstructing the methods of implementation and practical execution of the murder (i.e. the modus operands of the criminal action). Being able to establish the author's entry point on the crime scene and assess the difficulties that he encountered helps to deduce the killer's cunning and operational potential. It is important to be able to reconstruct the state of the crime scene at the time it was committed and to carry out the inspection at the same time as the killer acted. It is important to be able to evaluate the brightness, the present light, the noises of that moment and the environmental situation related to the transit of people from the crime scene. From the dynamics of the interaction between the author and the victim, the way of approaching the victim, the methods of attack and control can be reconstructed. Being able to reconstruct the victim's way of control helps a lot in defining not only the author's operational potential, but also his experiences with the crime, with previous crimes, with his knowledge of the laws and the judicial world. Being a very vast science, criminology has a huge field of action. Focusing on the aspects relating to the crime scene and therefore on the subject of crime, there many figures who operate and intervene first on the scene. Criminology, however, also benefits from the professionalism of laboratory and non-laboratory experts, who carry out their activities in relation to the science they are part of, offering an indispensable contribution for investigative activity.

The sciences closely related to criminology are:

- Forensic pathology;

- Forensic ballistics;

- Bloodstain Pattern Analysis;

- Forensic graphology;

- Forensic psychology.

We present below, in summary form, these subjects, before tackling them better in the continuation of the essay.

Forensic pathology

Forensic pathology is the science that uses the knowledge of medicine by making it available for the assessment of individual cases of judicial interest. Among the main figures of forensic pathology we mention:

- the coroner, who performs, among others, a very important function such as the autopsy, useful for tracing the times and causes of death.

- the forensic toxicologist, who studies the symptoms and causes of poisoning caused by drugs, drugs, poisons etc.

- the forensic anthropologist, who studies the skeletal remains and, together with the forensic odontology (which focuses on the jaw), tries to trace the sex of the victim by analyzing the remains, any abuse or mistreatment suffered and an approximate estimate of age.

- the forensic entomologist, who studies the life cycles of the various insects developed by the decomposition of the human body, useful for tracing the date of death.

Forensic Ballistics

Forensic ballistics is a science that deals with the study of firearms used in a crime. This science is useful for tracing the circumstances and dynamics of the crime, but also for reconstructing the distances in which the shot took place and the exact type of weapon used by the criminal.

Bloodstain Pattern Analysis

The Bloodstain Pattern Analysis (BPA) is the science that deals with the study of blood stains present at the crime scene, through the analysis of the arrangement of the spots and the morphology of the splashes. Thanks to this fascinating science, it is possible to trace the dynamics of aggression, any post mortem body movements and much more. The analysis of blood traces is a forensic science method suitable for analyzing the morphology of sketches, patches or bloodstains at the crime scene. The use of blood as evidence of the crime, however, is not new in criminology, although there are currently more advanced methods. The analysis is obtained thanks to scientific knowledge combined with other disciplines such as biology, chemistry, mathematics and physics. By following a pre-established analysis plan, it is possible to obtain excellent results with regard to scientific investigation. It is now a consolidated opinion that the analysis of traces of blood through a series of indicators can help investigators to clarify the investigation framework.

This science helps operators to understand the following determinations:

- movement of things or people while the crime was being committed;
- location of things or people during bleeding;
- movement of things or people after the crime;
- method or weapon used for the crime;
- splash direction;
- original area of impact "on" or "with" the body;
- the number of strokes made to carry out the crime;

The analysis of blood traces requires attention and considerable preparation, and it must be accompanied by other methods of investigation, which are not always taken for granted by the employees of the crime scene investigators.

Forensic Graphology

Forensic graphology is a science that investigates the psychological characteristics of a subject by analyzing its handwriting. For investigative purposes it is very useful for analyzing any letters, diaries, documents or various writings found at the crime scene. In some cases, this matter is fundamental also in the evidentiary context in the criminal trial. The validity and reliability of this technique have never been scientifically validated and its reliability is highly discussed. The investigation methodology starts from the assumption that writing, once the learning phases are over, becomes an automatic process, the result of motor responses to neurons. The graphic gesture, therefore, is interpreted as an "expressive gesture". Such behavioral responses can only be unique, as exclusive as the emotional experiences of individuals. From these premises would derive the possibility of interpretation of writing for the description of the human personality, an investigation that in the vision of the Morettian graphological school also includes the somatic aspect, both from a morphological and an expressive point of view. The use of "somatic graphology", however, is rather marginal in current research and practice. The graphologist must be aware of the mood and expectations of the subject when he writes; he tries to interpret the writer's mood based on the type of movement that underlies the graphic act. He studies the trait: lightness or heaviness, the curved or straight direction, the sharpness of the edges and so on. The graphologist must understand the state of spontaneity of the writer; in fact, the author often tends to disguise himself by imitating a model or trying to provide a certain self-image. The first principle is the analogy between character and writing; after all when we go to buy a dress we choose a suitable one, and therefore in some way similar to us, therefore the handwriting, as an intimate manifestation of man, can only be related to emotions and inevitably brings them to the surface. Another fundamental principle is symbolism, since subjects belonging to a certain culture share some fundamental symbols and the writing itself projects collective or individual symbols. The color of the sheet, the color of the stroke, can be a symbol of a precise mood. Graphology differs from calligraphic expertise in that graphology deals with the subject's personality, while calligraphic expertise is a scientific comparison of graphic signs in order to judicially establish its authenticity and traceability to the author. Calligraphic appraisals are conducted using precision instruments such as the digital stereoscopic microscope, in order to study the pressure of handwriting, which is an index to identify the author, as a person writing speed will never be able to emulate the graphic pressure of another. According to numerous publications, graphology would not be able to reliably determine the personological characteristics of the subject.

At various times, attempts to validate the graphological technique have given little or no results, which is why graphology is still not counted among the psychodiagnostic techniques but is recommended for use in personnel selection.

Forensic psychology

Forensic psychology is the branch of psychology that studies the psychological behavior of a criminal. It is a very vast science that has multiple fields of intervention both as regards the legal phase, through psychological appraisals, and as regards the investigative phase (such as the criminal profiling activity). Forensic psychology enjoys the wide contribution of other disciplines, such as criminal law and criminology and plays a primary role in understanding relevant judicial cases, in concert with other professional figures involved in the case.

An important aspect of this discipline, as we will soon see, is the study of the so-called "testimony psychology". The consultant's central function is to administer technical-psychological information to investigators through the use of a technical and repeatable lexicon. A lexicon that must be understandable even to those who are not psychologists: let's take the case of P.M. (Public Prosecutor) or the designated judge. In order to perform its technical role profitably, the forensic psychologist must know ethics, rules and legal practice. He must participate in the contradictory, even between the parties, and in his role, be able to discern what is technical and essential in the file and what is, instead, irrelevant. Even a minimal lack of skills can invalidate, without appeal, its credibility and usefulness to the process. In the various judicial systems, the questions asked by the magistrate to the forensic psychologist do not only concern psychological assessments to determine the defendant's ability to understand and want. The forensic psychologist also deals with matters of wider procedural relevance such as opinions on treatment or any other information requested by the judge. These tasks range from technical advice on the factors concomitant to the crime, to the risk of recidivism, to the reliability of the testimonies, to alternative measures to security detention, etc. His skills are also required in the training and accreditation of prison police staff, other sectors of the police force and in particular, in recent years, also of rescuers at the crime scene.

Special content: fighting without disintegrating

"Kills wife and takes life", "Kills husband and son", "Kills wife, mother-in-law and an innocent neighbor". How many times have you read such titles? Quarrels after quarrels that arise in tragedy. But is all this avoidable? In this bonus chapter we will tackle 12 ways to fight without disintegrating the other and ... end up on criminology manuals like this!

#1 Small pieces. Why bomb the other and tear him to pieces? Arguing is like disintegrating each other. Isn't this energy better destined for more ethical and pleasant activities?

#2 Tachycardia. Your heart beats a thousand, do you feel smoking and bubbling? Does this seem like the right time to fight? Are you sure? Wait when you are less crackling, remember you are a human being, not a popcorn. (!)

#3 Enemy. But is the other really your enemy? Isn't it something that resonates after witnessing the behavior you criticize? Could the other, given his degree of psycho-emotional development, behave differently? Think about it before you fight.

#4 One at a time. Really, can't you wait for the other to end? Do you have to overlap? Don't you think it's violent? One at a time, this is easier.

#5 Stop. What about a glass of water? A candy? A cookie? A ride around the house? In short, a break every now and then while arguing is not a crime. (!)

#6 Generic. Always. Never. All the women are ... All the men are ... All the in-laws are ... All the vegans are ... But do you need to generalize in this discussion?

#7 Stand on the piece. Is a glass falling? Well, stay on topic not to start from when your mother-in-law gave it to you at the wedding to quarrel on issues that have been suffered and discussed over years and years. (!)

#8 Insults. Beep, beep, beep, -------! Do you really think that insults are useful for discussions? Are you sure? Don't you think the other one closes and feels attacked and offended?

#9 In other people's shoes. Don't you understand each other? You feel misunderstood? Try to put on the other's boots or heels. Maybe you will understand that you don't need all this fighting.

#10 Sorry. Are you done fighting? Can't you take it anymore? Does the other apologize to you? How about accepting them? Don't you think it's an excellent idea?

#11 Honor of arms. Finished fighting? You still think you're right. Indeed, you are right and the other has just apologized to you? Well, do not drag his corpse as if you were Achilles with Ettore. Leave him a dignified surrender.

#12 Visions. Do you think this list is trivial, or worse, stupid? On the contrary, do you think it's brilliant? Whatever idea you have about it, you're right.

Chapter Three

"Crime Scene and forensic sciences"

"When I was a kid I used to pray every night for a new bicycle.
Then I realized that the Lord doesn't work that way so
I stole one and asked Him to forgive me."

EMO PHILIPS

Criminology is not an autonomous and self-sufficient discipline, but is part of many other sciences that deal with human nature and society. Indeed, any progress made in research into the causes of the crime must come from developments in these other branches of knowledge. Often too much time is wasted trying to find an elaborate and comprehensive definition of criminology, dividing and dividing its many branches of interest. At least twenty different terms are in use and form a confusing list: criminology, criminal science, criminal anthropology, criminal jurisprudence, criminal statistics, penology, prison science, penitentiary law, prison pedagogy, investigative science, crime and criminal profiling. It is not another definition that we need in this book, but a practical description of the functions. Take the heterogeneous composition of the population, the crowded urbanization of modern megacities, the intense mobility, the ever-growing temptations and opportunities, add new and disturbing dimensions to the crime phenomenon.

Criminology must thus face modernity, the fragmentation of social connections and the "wear and tear of modern life". Through the disciplines related to crime, we will try to understand how to deal with crimes and crime scenes. All this in the next few pages, knowing full well that for each chapter dealt with, an entire monograph dedicated to exhausting the current topic would not suffice.

Criminal psychology and investigative psychology can also be considered to belong to the criminal sciences, the former to the criminological sciences, and the latter to the forensic sciences. According to David Canter, founder of criminal and investigative psychology, psychology is directly applicable to the study of crime since crime must be viewed as a form of interpersonal relationship. In the case of the criminal act, this relationship is established between the criminal and the victim; therefore the modalities and motivations behind the criminal actions of a subject can be directly connected to those that accompany him in any other interpersonal relationship. One of the objectives of criminal and investigative psychology is to contribute to the definition of the so-called "psychological profile" of the possible author of a series of crimes, through a series of comparisons between investigative evidence (for example photographic findings) and psychological evidence-relational (the indicators of psychological and cognitive aspects of the person who committed the crime). This operation (which has become fashionable in many film and media productions, although it should be emphasized that there are not many real employment opportunities in the sector), is generally called criminal profiling (offender profiling or criminal profiling).

The field of criminal profiling, beyond its media fame, also due to successful television series (see Mindhunter's success on Netflix) however, remains a sector that, despite the intensity of studies and research, has provided few satisfactory results. Criminology is often confused by the mass media with "criminalistics", or with crime investigation, even if they are very distinct sectors.

While criminology is a science that studies crimes, offenders and possible measures to prevent, treat and control the crime, the investigation concerns activities aimed at finding out "who" has committed the crime in a specific way, put in place by the judicial police forces and by the defense of the suspect/accused of crimes, and criminalistics provide the same with the application methodologies for investigations, borrowed from the reference sciences (forensic sciences). Since the end of the nineteenth century, since the time of the discovery of fingerprints, criminalistics science has gone a long way. Today, for example, DNA analysis provides a new type of fingerprint, which allows to trace with remarkable levels of precision the identification of the perpetrator of some crimes. The chronicle shows that, more and more frequently, criminal cases are dealt with through sophisticated methodologies of investigation that draw from forensic sciences, that is, to those various disciplines that deal with the examination of traces found on the scene of a crime: forensic genetics , ballistics, toxicology, forensic medicine, electron microscopy. These sciences have nothing to do with criminology in the strict sense. In the process, these disciplines were increasingly relevant, often fundamental, to demonstrate the guilt of an offender or to exonerate an innocent person (also relative to distant and defined judicial facts); even if their claim to aspire to scientific "truth" has been repeatedly questioned by authoritative contributions. By entering with education and respect, but with a lot of curiosity, in the laboratories of modern criminalists, we will face another stage of this exciting journey into criminology.

Are you ready? Let's begin.

The crime scene can be any place, both indoors (e.g. a private home) and outdoors (e.g. a large shopping center). Each type of crime scene, together with the nature of the crime committed (robbery, murder, rape, arson, etc.) requires different investigation procedures. External crime scenes are the most problematic to investigate. Exposure to natural agents such as snow, rain, wind or heat, as well as to animal activity, contaminate the crime scene and lead to the destruction of evidence. Internal crime scenes are far less likely to be contaminated due to lack of exposure to the elements. Here, contamination usually occurs because of people: operators, onlookers and the same protagonists of the scene.

At the crime scene, photos of all the evidence are taken before something is touched, moved or analyzed. Generally, numbered markers are placed near each test to allow the organization of the clues. Making a sketch of the crime scene is also a form of documentation. This allows investigators to take notes as well as measure distances and other information that may not be easily deduced from a photograph. Investigators will ascertain the location of the evidence and all other objects in the room. The sketch is usually drawn looking from above, which can also be useful like all other activities to obtain evidence. Generic diagnosis represents the first step, mandatory and indifferent, of the medical-legal laboratory investigation. Here, it is ascertained, for example, if a reddish spot is of a blood nature (i.e. if it is blood), if a yellowish consists of saliva, sperm or urine, if a fiber is natural (fragment of dress or hair) or artificial . Various tests are carried out for these checks. First guidelines or preliminary and, subsequently, tests of scientific certainty. The orientation tests are used as preliminary screening, being very sensitive (they are carried out with really small quantities of material), but not as specific. It is therefore necessary to carry out subsequent tests as well.

The confirmation of the presence of blood, sperm, vaginal fluids, saliva, when possible, is obtained with techniques that give the certainty of the nature and the category the finding. These investigations are very reliable but have the disadvantage of requiring a fair amount of material, which can sometimes compromise subsequent identification investigations, which are extremely more sensitive. Generally speaking, there are four methods for determining the presence of blood or sperm:

- the visual method;

- the physical method;

- the chemical method;

- the microscopic method.

Apart from the visual method, each of these can give results of orientation or scientific certainty. The visual method, immediately and directly implemented, represents the preliminary phase which, even today, allows you to direct the search for traces to be subjected to subsequent laboratory tests. It should never be forgotten that the bloodstains can take on various color scales ranging from red to brown, up to dark green. Those of sperm from white to grayish, to yellowish, with edges typically "geographic", while those of saliva or sweat can be completely invisible macroscopically. The traces of sperm, but also of saliva, sweat, urine and other biological liquids, become visible in ultraviolet light or with the use of light sources at specific wavelengths, associated with appropriate lenses.

They are of particular use when large surfaces have to be explored, with the result of making the spot appear luminescent. The microscopic examination assumes particular importance in the search for sperm, when the sperm cells whose characteristics are completely peculiar are highlighted. If there is a simple suspicion that on a substrate (e.g. an undergarment) there may be an invisible trace, it is possible to resort to chemical techniques that allow, in most cases, to detect its presence. Among the chemical methods for the blood nature, the tests based on the properties of the blood pigment should be mentioned. On a similar principle there are the tests that allow to detect the presence of even small quantities of blood because it is washed or very diluted (for example the catalytic test of Luminol), extremely sensitive, but also non-specific and, above all, their profiles of repeatability of the assessment are far from obvious.

The generic diagnosis of saliva, however, is made through the demonstration of amylase in the trace. Amylase is an enzyme produced by pancreatic cells that promotes the digestion of food in the body. However, amylase is not only produced by the pancreas, but also by the salivary glands and, in women, by the fallopian tubes. For the diagnosis of feces, apart from the morphological and organoleptic characteristics, it is necessary to resort to tests that highlight the presence of urobilinogen or other faecal pigments. For the diagnosis of urine, apotryptophanase or tryptophanase is demonstrated with appropriate reagents or, more easily, by demonstrating the high concentration of urea and creatinine. Microcrystallographic tests are also part of the chemical methods which consist in determining, through appropriate reagents, the formation of characteristic crystals both in the case of the blood stain (certainty test for the diagnosis of blood), and in that of sperm where, however, they do not allow the diagnosis of certainty, which is obtained instead with the microscopic investigation.

Chromatographic tests on paper or on thin substrate can currently be considered the method of choice for the general diagnosis of blood, even on minimal traces. As for the investigations on hair, they are very frequent, given the ease with which this finding can be transferred from one place to another due to natural fall, to have been torn or to have remained on, for example, clothing. The investigations on hair, however, present problems similar to those relating to any other trace: that is, a generic, specific, individual, regional diagnosis may be required.

The generic diagnosis is performed by observation with an optical microscope to detect the fundamental characteristics of the piliferous structure, i.e. the presence of a root, a stem and an end. Often, the limited amount of biological material available requires complex choices that can involve the sacrifice of the important preliminary step of generic diagnosis in favor of individual genetic diagnosis.

Fact that realizes the apparent scientific paradox on the basis of which it is possible to identify with certainty a subject as "donor" of a track without it has been possible to establish the exact nature of the starting biological material. Once the nature of a stain has been identified, it is necessary to determine whether it is of human or animal nature (so-called diagnosis: species/specific). If the size of the trace allows it, the techniques still more used today for the diagnosis of species are immunological (immunodiffusion) which allow to compare an extract from the trace in question with different serums containing anti-human, anti-horse, dog antibodies , cat, etc. and to observe the formation of a band of precipitate in correspondence with the specific antiserum. Alternatively, methods that employ monoclonal antibodies against humans, dogs, cats, etc. are also commonly used with techniques aimed at the determination of antigens.

These techniques involve:

- Adhesion. A primary antibody is placed on the bottom of the plate well which will be the specific one for the antigen to be searched.

- Washing, to eliminate the antibodies that have not bound to the plate.

- The serum that should contain the antigen is added inside the well. If the antigen is present, this will bind with the primary antibody bound to the bottom of the plate.

- Washing, to eliminate the serum.

- Addition of a solution containing a secondary antibody that carries an enzyme bound. The secondary antibody will bind to the antigen (if this is present).

- Washing, to eliminate the secondary antibody that has not bound the antigen.

- Addition of a specific substrate for the enzyme linked to the secondary antibody. If the enzyme is present (and therefore the secondary antibody is present and therefore if the antigen is present) this will convert the substrate into a colored compound. The diagnosis of species on hair formations is generally performed by microscopic examination. In fact, the cuticle, i.e. the outer layer of the hair formation, the cortical substance, containing the pigment granules, and the medullary, i.e. the central portion that may be present, absent or in clods, have peculiar characteristics that easily allow the diagnosis of human or animal species. There are also more sophisticated genetic techniques, which provide for the examination of the mitochondrial DNA, also achievable on hair/hair; they are extremely sensitive and specific but have the disadvantage of invasiveness (and therefore the high cost), and are most often used not by forensic doctors but by zoologists. The question of the origin of a trace from a certain body district (regional diagnosis) concerns the piliferous formations and the traces of blood, since the generic diagnosis, for other biological materials, immediately identifies its origin. The regional morphological (macro/microscopic) diagnosis of hair, axillary hair, pubic hair, etc., based solely on the dimensional data (length, thickness) and on the shape of the section (round or oval), is far from providing elements of certainty. Various criteria apply to express general assessments regarding the origin of a blood spot: that is, we take into account the results of the somatic examination of the individual from whom the blood is said to originate, the characteristics of the site, of the amplitude, of the shape of the stains, and finally the microscopic examination of the material constituting them.

Evidently, in order to have hemoptysis, respiratory tract injuries are required; to have a hemorrhoid hemorrhage, the existence of hemorrhoids is necessary; a woman who has passed menopause will not be able to attribute the spots to her own menstruation, etc. The location of the distribution of bloodstains, especially on clothing, as well as on bed linen, and elsewhere, can also be significant elements. More recent methods provide for the evaluation of tissue-specific gene expression by analyzing ribonucleic acid (RNA), which has unique characteristics for that specific tissue or cell type. A limitation of this analysis lies in the overall lower resistance of the RNA to degradation compared to the DNA: for this reason this approach may not allow any result on particularly scarce and/or degraded biological materials.

Chapter Four
"Tools of the modern criminologist"

"The very emphasis of the commandment:
Thou shalt not kill, makes it certain that we are
descended from an endlessly long chain of generations of
murderers,
whose love of murder was in their blood as it is perhaps also in
ours."
SIGMUND FRUED

Forensic DNA

We have all heard, at least once in a lifetime, of DNA profile (also called DNA fingerprinting, DNA testing, or DNA typing). DNA detection is a forensic technique used to identify individuals with characteristics of their DNA. A DNA profile is an agglomeration of variations of deoxyribonucleic or deoxyribonucleic acid that is different in all unrelated individuals, therefore being as unique to individuals as are fingerprints (hence the alternative name for the technique). The DNA profile should not be confused with complete genome sequencing. Developed from the beginning in 1985, the DNA profile is used, for example, for family tests and criminal investigations, to identify a person or to put a person in a crime scene; those techniques are now used globally in science forensics to facilitate police investigations and help clarify controversial paternity and immigration practices. The modern DNA profiling process was developed in 1988 and increasingly perfected over time. Forensic medicine uses DNA, generally isolated from blood, skin, saliva, hair and other biological tissues and fluids, to identify those responsible for crimes or violence. The process used is genetic fingerprinting: this technique consists in comparing the length of the variable sections of the repetitive DNA, such as short tandem repeats and minisatellites, which can be very different between one individual and another.

The comparison between two DNA samples under examination is therefore not based on the analysis of the entire deoxyribonucleotide sequence, but only on these sections. In fact, two individuals not related by kinship relationships have in common 99.9% of DNA sequence. This method is usually very reliable, although sometimes the identification of criminals can be complicated if the scene is contaminated by the DNA of several people. This method, developed in 1984 by British geneticist Sir Alec Jeffreys, was first used in 1988 to incriminate suspect Colin Pitchfork. In 1983, the body of a 15-year-old student, Lynda Mann, was found near Narborough, a small town in Leicestershire in the English Midlands. Lynda went to visit a friend of hers and never returned home. After two days the girl's body was found; it showed clear signs of strangulation and sexual violence. Police investigations led to nothing, but all the evidence was collected and cataloged, including biological evidence left by the murderer on the corpse.

About three years later Dawn Ashworth, also a fifteen-year-old student, disappeared from home and was later found strangled and raped in the same wooded area where the previous murder had been committed. The girl had taken a shortcut from school instead of taking her usual route but, as the police suspected, her assailant, believing he had "got away" once, had committed the murder in the same way. Also in this case biological traces were collected on the corpse of the young student. The ways in which the violence and murder were perpetrated led the police to believe that they were the result of a single homicidal rapist. The police focused their suspicions on a young local man, Richard Buckland, a 17-year-old boy with learning difficulties who had been spotted near Dawn Ashworth's murder scene. In addition, the boy appeared to be aware of details about the discovery of the girl's body, which the police had never revealed. After several interrogations, the young man confessed to the murder of the second girl, but denied any involvement in the murder three years earlier.

At that point, the police requested the assistance of Sir Alec Jeffreys, an expert in DNA analysis. Jeffreys, at 09:05 on Monday 10 September 1984, had what the Anglo-Saxons call "eureka moment". In his laboratory in Leicester he faced an experiment and, looking at the image of a DNA film, he realized that it showed both the similarities and the differences between the DNA of different members of the family of one of his technicians. In about half an hour, he realized the possible scope of DNA as fingerprinting, which uses the variations in the genetic code of each individual. Jeffreys accepted the request and, in collaboration with the scientists of the English Forensic Science Service, compared the DNA profiles obtained from the sperm samples taken from the crime scenes and the one obtained from a blood sample taken from the only suspect, and shortly after he handed over his results to the police. The two rapes were the result of one man's work, but this man was not Richard Buckland. A giant manhunt started in search of the subject whose genetic profile corresponded to that of the violence.

All adult male individuals in the area were asked to spontaneously donate a sample of their blood for comparison. Obviously a refusal would have attracted the police suspects and therefore about 5000 blood samples were analyzed. However, even this enormous effort was useless and no trace of the murderer was found. It was then assumed that the killer was not resident in those areas, but an individual passing through. Just when all hopes of finding the culprit seemed to have vanished, a witness said he heard a man in a pub bragging that he had provided a blood sample instead of a friend, Colin Pitchfork, who had asked him for a favor. Colin Pitchfork was a young baker in the village, and had asked his friend for the favor, because being he on bail for a conviction for obscene acts, he said, he would certainly have been accused and framed by the Police.

He managed to convince his friend that he had nothing to do with the deaths of the two girls. The police immediately went to him and collected his DNA. His genetic profile was the same as those obtained from both crime scenes. Pitchfork confessed to both murders, telling the most heinous details. But who was Colin Pitchfork? He was a married man, father of two children, and was twenty-three years old at the time of the events. Before his marriage he had been convicted of obscene acts and was in therapy at a hospital center. He worked as a baker, and was particularly skilled as a sculptor of cake decorations and for this he was highly esteemed in the town, especially by children. His boss claimed that he was: "a very good worker, who met deadlines but had to be kept from working with female staff because he was a little moody". During the interrogation he admitted that he had a sort of "compulsion" towards women, which was manifested to him when he was only a boy and this pushed him to commit obscene acts. Even in the case of the two girls, they ran away when he had approached them and this had excited him, then he killed them for fear of being reported. Young Buckland and the baker Pitchfork were the first two suspects to experiment with the use of the DNA profile in a courtroom. The first, seeing his innocence demonstrated, the second, seeing his guilt definitively proven. In 1988 Colin Pitchfork was sentenced to life imprisonment, with a sentence of thirty years for the violence and murder of the two girls. In current practice, suspects are often asked to provide a DNA sample for comparison with any biological findings present at the crime scene. Furthermore, sad news in these times of international terrorism, genetic fingerprinting can also be used to identify the victims of mass accidents.

In terms of DNA, there is a particular forensic extraction procedure. In fact, in order to be analyzed, the DNA must be extracted from the trace or the reference sample and purified from the proteins and substances that may have been present on it (e.g. dust, soil, fibers of clothing, etc.). The step of determining the quantity and quality of the extracted DNA is necessary in order to be able to adjust the quantity necessary for the subsequent phases, now carried out almost exclusively by means of the chain polymerization reaction (PCR) technique.

The study of DNA polymorphisms in the forensic field is carried out by comparing genetic structures. For example, the profile of the DNA extracted from the blood trace present on the suspect's pants with that extracted from the blood of the victim, or the profile of the DNA extracted from the seminal fluid taken from the victim of sexual violence with that of a possible investigated person. The result that derives from this can be of complete discrepancy between two genetic structures, or of compatibility, but not of identity. The question that is usually asked of the forensic geneticist is whether a certain individual can be excluded as the one who left the trace on the crime scene. While, as mentioned, the answer to the first part of the question can be very quick, due to the complete incompatibility between two genetic profiles, the answer to the second is not as simple. And, on this aspect, the cases of judicial reporting have spent many words. An answer to this question, in fact, passes through an evaluation of the frequency in the reference population (Italian, Dutch, English, etc.) of the phenotype (genotype), obtained from the examination of each system which leads to a cumulative frequency value, which in turn reveals the greater or lesser rarity of the profile. The reciprocal of this frequency value represents the number of subjects in the reference population who randomly share the same genetic profile.

Values of 1 in 10,000, 1 in 100,000 are rapidly giving way to extremely more significant values, such as those of 1 out of several billion or more, thanks to the possibility of using increasingly informative genetic systems, or with very low cumulative frequencies. Therefore, in carrying out the investigations, the genetic systems used, i.e. those with greater discriminative capacity than others, are of fundamental importance. The DNA test, for several years now, has proven to be completely reliable and usable even in delicate investigations in the forensic field, provided that the relevant quality standards are respected through the guidelines and directives that at various levels are issued by international and national scientific communities. The goal of maximum reliability is achieved through a specific preparation of those who work there (laboratory managers, technicians, etc.), through suitable structures and machinery, and also through the use of operating techniques that have the approval of the international scientific community: the genetic systems used, in fact, must prove to be sufficiently reliable, informative, transmissible according to the rules of Mendelian segregation (relative to the use in paternity investigations) and must be accompanied by an adequate set of frequency data in the population.

Weapons and forensic ballistics

Forensic ballistics is based on the principle that all firearms are characterized by indelible, unique differences, due to the heterogeneous mechanism with which they are manufactured. Forensic ballistics represents a link between the science of the motion of a bullet, or that particular branch of physics with links to mathematics, chemistry and law (Criminal Process, Criminal Law and Criminal Procedure). In cases where a firearm has been used, with consequent injuries or death, a correct medical-legal diagnosis, although based on the careful examination of the "basic" data (number of shots exploded, firing distance and mutual position between the victim and the victim), may sometimes prove incomplete or insufficient in the absence of an integrated assessment with the results of investigations commonly considered to be of a more exquisitely criminal nature: the examination of the weapon and its mechanics, the definition of the number of shots unexploded in the magazine, identification of the caliber of the exploded projectiles, and interpretation of environmental and testimonial findings. The forensic ballistics investigations for the identification and description of the place where the event occurred; the examination of damage by ballistic agent in environments and on vehicles; the search, collection, conservation and identification of the finds of ballistic interest; examination of the weapon, verification of its characteristics and functionality;

identification of the shooter; firing distance evaluation. In addition to these, in proposing reconstructive hypotheses of the event, due consideration should be given to the medico-legal issues regarding the assessment of the time of death and/or injury, the cause and the means used, such as example survival time and the possibility of autonomously carrying out actions or displacements after injury, type or types of weapon used, caliber, number of shots, firing distance and mutual position between victim and shooter. However, forensic ballistics suffers from certain difficulties of analysis with particular types of weapons whose projectiles flow through plastic patinas which prevent their contact with the barrel. For this type of weapon there are other analyzes that can reveal its sources. In cases where a firearm has been used, resulting in injury or death of the act, a (correct) medical-legal diagnosis, although based on the careful examination of the "basic factual" data (number of shots exploded views, shooting distance and mutual position between actor and victim), can often prove incomplete or non-exhaustive. This is true in cases where there is an absence of an evaluation accompanied by investigations commonly considered to be of a more exquisitely criminal nature, such as: the examination of the weapon and its mechanics, the definition of the number of unexploded shots in the magazine, identification of the caliber of the exploded projectiles, as well as the interpretation of environmental and testimonial findings.

Forensic ballistics therefore means everything that has in any way to do with the attempted or actual use, direct or indirect, of a firearm.

The weapon in question may be known or not. We too, for didactic - scientific and exhibition reliability, have classified the areas of competence of the ballistic investigation into four categories: "internal ballistics"; "analysis of weapons in general"; "technology analysis" and "motion of the bullets inside the barrel". Internal ballistics analyzes the transformation of the chemical energy of a powder into mechanical energy (mainly kinetic), due to the propulsion of a projectile. Internal ballistics studies the phenomena that occur from the moment the cartridge is fired until the moment the bullet comes out of the weapon's mouth. The next phase, as mentioned above, becomes the object of study of external ballistics. Following the violent action of the firing pin on the trigger capsule, the primer composition is compressed against the anvil of the capsule (in the case of annular percussion, the trigger is crushed against the metal of the bottom edge). The composition detonates producing an intense blazing lightning that, through the holes of the trigger, reaches the charge of dust, giving way to its explosion. This will be more or less fast in relation to the priming force, the type, conformation and quantity of the powder, the loading density (ratio between the volume of the powder and the space in the cartridge), the compression exerted on the powder, the force with which the bullet is held by the cartridge case and many other variables. The dust must be able to completely burn before the bullet comes out of the barrel, both because in this way all the energy is used, and to prevent the residues from igniting outside the muzzle of the weapon (blaze of muzzle). External ballistics deals with the analysis of the motion of the projectile in the external space between the muzzle of the weapon and the target or the point of fall. In the external space the projectile follows a trajectory which is the result of three distinct forces: the initial impulse which gives it a uniform and straight motion, the resistance of the air which opposes it in the opposite direction, and the force of gravity which tends to drop the bullet towards the ground with uniformly accelerated motion. Air resistance plays an important role for fast projectiles and therefore, for very slow projectiles (ancient artillery, arrows, stones) it can be almost neglected. Think, in a purely exemplifying sense, that for a nineteenth-century mortar the difference compared to the trajectory in the void was only 10%. External ballistics therefore analyzes the "conduct" and trajectory of all bodies launched into space up to their point of impact; it includes the measurement and calculation of the velocity of the bullet at the exit from the barrel. What does terminal ballistics do instead? It deals with the analysis of the effects of bullets, cartridge elements, fragments and splinters on the animated target (man and animal) or on inanimate raw material.

Terminal ballistics therefore analyzes the "behavior" of the bullet when it reaches the target and the consequent physiological and biological reactions in the affected living body. In other words, terminal ballistics studies the behavior of the bullet in the target. One of the phenomena that best lends itself to a scientific study is that of the penetration of the projectile into the various media, while considering that the diversity of materials and the diversity of behavior of the individual projectiles, according to their structure and speed at the moment of impact, do not allow the use of a general mathematical model, but only empirical formulas.

That is to concrete cases, which can be analyzed from time to time. It happens in fact, on one hand, that high-speed projectiles are easily deformed on impact and, on the other hand, that very fast projectiles do not have time to transfer their energy to the target! Fundamental, in this field of forensic study, is the autopsy aimed at determining the causes and methods of the death of the victim, estimating the shooting distance, the dynamics of the crime event; for this reason it is absolutely necessary, as well as good practice, that the forensic doctor be assisted by an expert in forensic ballistics. The "ballistics of injuries" is also of considerable importance for the coroner, for the ballistic expert and for the criminalist, in the analysis of some crimes and the understanding of the related harmful phenomena, in order to deny or confirm hypotheses and testimonies and to carry out a scientific reconstruction of the dynamics of the crime event.

Terminal ballistics also plays an important role in the construction of fireproof protections (armoring of vehicles, construction of Kevlar bulletproof vests, etc.). Given this premise, let's try to sketch a conclusion and an overall look at the matter. Internal, external and terminal ballistics merge and materialize in the broad theoretical-operational field of the so-called identification ballistics. This science deals, among other things, with analysis, technical evaluation and microscopic comparison of ballistic finds, with the identification and study of the weapon used in a criminal event starting from the exact metric-morphological data of ballistic finds found on the crime scene. It also deals with the decoding of the marks of the weapons and the reconstruction of the worn or obliterated registration marks, and the analysis of the GSR shot residues following the deflagration of a cartridge. But that's not all, the identification ballistics addresses the estimation of the firing distance starting from both the evaluation of the density of any shot residues found on certain subjects and/or their clothing and from the analysis of the terminal ballistic lesions on the victim and the ballistic characteristics of the weapon used. It also deals with the dynamics of the event and the examination of the crime scene, the computerized three-dimensional reconstruction of the crime scene and the dynamics of the crime event in order to identify the epicentres of fire, the trajectories of the bullets and the reciprocal positions (shooter - victim - eyewitnesses) so as to scientifically succeed in denying or confirming hypotheses and testimonials and much more. Investigations on gunshot residues are also included in this area. It is an intriguing and fascinating science, very technological, still evolving both on the interpretation of data and on the research itself that deals with it. The illustrious scholar Gonzales in the 1930s was the first to take an interest in and establish a particular method for identifying the gunshot residues on the suspect's hands. He identified a procedure that involved the spreading of melted paraffin, therefore very hot, on the hands of the suspects. The fact that it was very hot should have, in theory, dilated the pores of the suspect's epidermis and captured any particles present on the hand, both burned and unburned. The final cooled product, called paraffin glove, was subjected to a chemical investigation called Diphenylamine. The end result of this research, in the case of positivity, was that the residues were colored blue. However, it was then shown that this coloring was achieved also in the presence of urine (nitrites and nitrates) and fertilizers, etc. During investigations into the murder of President Kennedy in the United States, methods were developed to ascertain the presence of metal residues resulting from the detonation of the priming mixture: lead styphnate, barium dioxide, antimony sulfide, etc. technical research guidelines. In the forensic world, and more generally in the scientific universe, even a few years can lead to major changes. Two important events in this area are briefly reported below. On February 15, 2007, the ASTM (standard specification) approved a new release of the GSR standard called E 1588.

In addition to numerous other changes compared to the previous version, one of the most significant innovations was the definitive de-classification of compatible features. In October of the same year, the 15th International Forensic Science Symposium organized by Interpol was held in Lyon. In this congress the criteria and guidelines already established during the F.B.I. Symposium of 2005 and some other works published by researchers in the meantime. For professionals, this means that an important change has occurred in the operating techniques, protocols and evaluation of the results obtained. An important element of probative validity for the purpose of identifying the offender, where a firearm has been used, is the search for the residuals of the shot. The interest attributed to this means of investigation is of considerable technical relevance as the science itself is reduced to types of assessments considered insecure, doubtful and quarrelsome that did not allow, in fact, to ascertain in "science and consciousness" the presence or absence of particles resulting from the deflagration of ammunition.

During the firing of a firearm, the considerable pressure and temperature of the combustion gases inside the barrel, on one hand, causes the projectile to escape, while on the other it causes chemical-physical reactions on very small particles of gunpowder. The latter are projected out of the same weapon and invest the surrounding surfaces in the form of aerosols. Generally speaking, in the cartridges there are two types of gunpowder: the trigger powder that transforms the mechanical energy of percussion into thermo-chemical energy, which is subsequently transferred to the launch powder: the launch powder that creates the bullet propulsion. As components of the trigger it is customary to find: barium, nitrate, lead, calcium, silicide, antimony, sulphide etc.

The material most commonly used for the manufacture of the cartridge cases is brass Cu-Zn 35 (the number indicates the percentage of zinc present). Aluminum, zinc, copper and some types of plastics are also used in the manufacturing of the cases. As far as bullets are concerned, they can consist of only lead, or have the central part (core) in lead and an external coating (shell) in copper or antimony or nickel. The residues of the shot, therefore, can be constituted not only by elements coming from the triggers, but also by those that derive from the external coating of the bullet and from the edge of the cartridge case.

When the deflagration takes place inside the combustion chamber of a weapon, three phases occur in a few seconds. A first phase (so-called pyrostatic) characterized by the combustion of the throwing powder at a constant volume, since the projectile is stationary. In this phase, the temperature reaches 2,000°C and the pressure reaches 1,400 p.s.i. (pound square inch = pound x square inch); a second phase (so-called pyrodynamics), characterized by the contemporaneity of constant volume combustion and variable pressures. The temperature and pressure reach the maximum levels: around 3,600 ° C and around 40,000 p.s.i. A final and third phase (so-called expansion) characterized by the expansion of the gas and the motion of the projectile.

The three phases occur almost simultaneously with the detonation of the trigger. As already mentioned, metallic elements such as iron, antimony and barium, which are part of the chemical composition of the trigger powders, during firing (as well as other metallic elements which are part of the chemical composition of the throwing powder, due to the high thermal and mechanical energy and the high pressure to which they are subjected) undergo a process of fusion and subsequent vaporization, thus finding themselves present together in the form of melted droplets (aerosols) which immediately cool down coming to often, but not always, take on a characteristic spheroidal appearance, similar to the phenomenon of volcanic boluses; that's way they have been called fireballs.

The shape and composition of these residues, called **GSR** (Gun Shot Residue) or **CDR** (Cartridge Discharge Residue), which come from the priming powder during the shot, is such as to leave no doubt for investigation purposes. In fact, human activities other than firing that can produce particles containing lead (Pb), barium (Ba) and antimony (Sb) are not known at present. Their diameter usually ranges from 0.5 to 50 microns. Persistence times are important elements for identification, interpretation and conclusions. Due to the force of gravity, the number of particles present on a given surface is destined to decrease over time. We are talking about the relationship between the number of hours and the number of particles. It is evident that the use of the various types of weapons necessarily affects the quantity of particles present on the person under investigation (short weapon, long weapon, etc.). The shape and diameter are very influential for the conclusions. For example, finding a large particle after a time span of many hours is a negative element, precisely because the large particles are the first to fall due to the force of gravity.

Fingerprints and dactyloscopy

The skin that covers the entire human body, the epidermis, is made up of five layers from the inside to the outside of the body, characterized by a greater state of keratinization: stratum basale, stratum spinosum, stratum granulosum, stratum lucidum, and stratum corneum. The basal or germinativum layer is composed of small and very thickened cells, arranged in palisade on the membrane in contact with the dermis. The cells of this layer reproduce and are pushed towards the surface to form the next layer, which is called "spiny" or "Malpighi". Said layer is formed by coarsely polyhedral shaped cells, more flattened than those of the basal layer and separated from each other by intercellular substance.

The surfaces of the palms of the hands, the soles of the feet and the inside of the phalanges, are characterized by a particular structure such as the dermal papillae, which determine the formation of the skin crests, which are small fleshy reliefs that contain the Messner's tactile corpuscles. The papillae, which reach the outermost surface, have tiny sweat pores that secrete a transparent substance composed of water, sodium chloride, potassium carbonate, volatile fatty acids, sulphates, etc., so, if the skin crests come into contact with a more or less smooth surface, they deposit the substance secreted by them, determining the formation of an impression, mirroring their design. A fingerprint is a trace left by the dermatoglyphs of the last phalanx of the fingers. A dermatoglyph is instead the result of the alternation of ridges and furrows. Dermatoglyphs are present on the palms of the hands, on the soles of the feet and on the fingertips. The crests vary in width from 100 to 300 microns, while the furrow period corresponds to approximately 500 microns. Dactyloscopy is the branch of criminalistics that studies papillary skin crests, mainly of the fingertips, in order to identify the offender, based on the prints left by him at the crime scene. It should be noted that the application of dactyloscopy to identify the offender allows for an indirect search for identity, which is obviously relative and not absolute.

The mathematician Balthazard established a system of recognition and comparison of the fingerprints which was based on an exponential type of empirical formula; he hypothesized that between two fingerprints there could have been just seventeen points of correspondence, on a series of seventeen billion one hundred seventy-nine million (17,179,000,000) of specimens! In practice, a possibility out of tens of billions that a fingerprint fragment, containing seventeen characteristic marks, may have been deposited by a person other than that to which it is attributed: if we consider that the world population is only a few billion individuals however, distributed over the entire surface of the globe, this occurrence can reasonably be considered at least unlikely. A statistically improbable event does not necessarily have to be considered impossible with absolute certainty. However, in the case of fingerprints, the differentiating elements are such and so many, that an unlikely event can practically be considered impossible. Two fingerprints left by the same individual will never be perfectly superimposable; in fact, the identity between two fingerprints is determined not by the perfect overlap, but by the coincidence of the shape of the papillary bundles and by a high number of points of detail.

Fragments of fingerprints, even very small, would provide numerous elements of evidence if we used poroscopy, suggested by Edmond Locard, which is based on the examination of the pores of the fingertip crests. Poroscopy is the last frontier of the papillary investigation and allows us to uniquely identify a trace from the morphology of the pore on the epidermis. It is evident, in fact, that in a fingerprint the quantity of identifiable identification points is proportional to the surface that can be examined: the smaller it is, the less likely it is to ascertain a sufficient number of particularities on it, or to obtain identification of the person to whom it belongs. The application of poroscopy, i.e. the study of the position of the sweat pores, would lead to a significant reduction in the minimum area necessary for identification tests. The first court case that was solved thanks to the fingerprints of the culprit dates back to about a century ago. The fingertips and palms of our hands (and also of the feet) are sprinkled with tiny conical shaped papillae that follow one after the other forming thin crests separated by small furrows.

The crests describe characteristic, absolutely individual designs (lugs, arches, vortices), that two monovular twins have the same DNA, but different fingerprints. The papillary crests are formed during the twelfth week and are completed after the sixth month of intrauterine life; they are also preserved in corpses, as long as epidermal support exists. The papillary crests do not undergo transformations over the life of an individual, except in special cases, in which they themselves constitute salient marks for the identification of a person. The fingerprints are different from individual to individual and, in the same individual, the traces left by the ten fingers are all different from each other. On the classifiability of fingerprints, which can be traced back to the four basic types of figure, namely delta, monodelta, bidelta and mixed. The papillary designs, in fact, do not alter their morphology during the individual's life, that is, they remain unchanged from the moment of their formation, around the third month of intrauterine life, until the onset of putrefactive phenomena following death, except in the case of traumatic effects (for example, deep removal of the dermis), or following particular infectious skin diseases. The epidermis is layered on the dermatoglyphs contained on the lower layers of the dermis and therefore fingerprints are also reconstructed in case of lesions on the skin.

Elements of forensic archeology

In less than a hundred years, the classic figure of the archaeologist has changed radically. In fact, the modern "Indiana Jones" have specialized more and more, appropriating techniques and applications pertinent to multiple scientific disciplines, serving them to their needs. Forensic archeology is a sector of judicial archeology that concerns the use of reading techniques and interpretation of the material traces and contexts of the archaeological discipline in the medical-legal field. The forensic archaeologist deals in particular in the analysis of a crime scene for the recognition and classification of the finds, the identification of their origin and era, and for the reconstruction of the spatial arrangement of people or objects in a given place and moment and the temporal sequence of anthropic and natural actions occurred. The acquisition of new scientific techniques applied to archeology has allowed the archaeologist to work also in the forensic field, making his specialization available to investigators both in contexts related to crime scenes, and to those related to other areas such as mass accidents (for example due to plane crashes) or cases of mass burials. The first state to employ archaeologists to search for human remains was the United Kingdom: in 1988 the discovery of the body of a minor, Stephen Jennings, by a team of forensic archaeologists, in fact marked the beginning of a close collaboration between investigating authorities and forensic archaeologists in cadaveric concealment scenarios.

Forensic archeology is now called to answer questions relating to the concealment of bodies, weapons, drugs, stolen goods, etc. and identification and possible excavation in the event of mass burials in wartime. The illustrious scientist John Hunter was the first author who in "Forensic Archeology: Advances in Theory and Practice" (2001) exposed the questions to which the competence of the forensic archaeologist can give answers. In Europe and in the world the presence of the forensic archaeologist is generally required in two cases:

1. excavation of an underground burial discovered accidentally;

2. targeted research, following judicial police investigations, and in case of discovery, excavation of a burial. When human remains are found ("clandestine burial"), the presence of a forensic doctor and, in the case of skeletal remains, the forensic anthropologist are also required. The archaeologist will therefore have to stop all excavation operations until the arrival of the latter with whom he will have to work in a team under the direction of a public prosecutor.

In case of concealment of a buried corpse immediately after death, by excavating archaeologically, a series of investigations may be carried out to establish the period to which the underground tomb dates. The stratigraphic sciences, in which archaeologists are experts, will be able to provide indications on the terminus ante quem by analyzing the layers that cover the pit, and on the terminus post quem by analyzing the stratigraphy cut by the underground tomb and the material inside. In fact, in case of superficial fortuitous discoveries, it is not always obvious that it is a corpse buried inside a pit. This is why it is necessary to consult a forensic archaeologist, so that his correct reading of the stratigraphic sequence of the soil can determine if we are in the presence of an old tomb, a hidden corpse, or something else. The preservation of the integrity of the burial carried out by the forensic anthropologist (specialized in the preservation of the finds) will allow the coroner and the anthropologist to perform a detailed examination of the body on the site of the discovery, provided that the original configuration of the corpse has not been compromised by the excavation. In conclusion, the relationship between science and law is a fascinating and at the same time insidious and complex thing. It is not a question of sterile and purely theoretical importance, but of events which have their practical repercussions and which concern the lives of many people. Just think of the decisions that a magistrate makes on the basis of the so-called "scientific evidence". The forensic sciences are nothing but the set of a broad spectrum of scientific disciplines applied to the field of law. The term "forensic science" is so vast, in fact, that includes an infinite number of scientific disciplines. But it is in the methods and objectives that science and law differ dramatically. Science aims to achieve the objective, authentic truth. The law, however, more prosaically, is satisfied with the "procedural" truth.

In the courts, in fact, a judge or a jury establishes what the "truth" is, and truth lies in what they themselves deliberate, that is the "procedural truth". Despite this, those involved in forensic science know that team work with other experts (investigators, magistrates, lawyers, etc.) is essential to bring the truth closer and serve justice.

Special content: The history of fingerprints

In the eighteenth century, in France, the intellectuals of the time believed that the coercive system of branding inmates was unnecessarily cruel, for this reason an anthropometric detection system began to be developed. William Herschel was probably the first researcher who thought of using the prints of the palms of the hands and fingertips in personal signaling. Fingerprints were also used by the Romans: it seems that Saint Paul signed his letters with his fingerprint; they were also used in China and, more recently, in India by the British.

Some archaeological finds show that dermatoglyphs and, in particular, fingerprints were used in the past as a form of personal identification. In the Roman Empire, fingerprints were used for identification purposes. In Persia, in the 14th century, by looking at several official documents that had been signed with fingerprints, an officer noted that there are no exactly two identical prints. In 1686 Marcello Malpighi, professor of anatomy at the University of Bologna, analyzed ridge lines, whorls and loops in one of his treatises, but did not emphasize the importance of fingerprints for personal identification purposes. John Evangelist Purkinji, professor of anatomy at the University of Breslau, in 1823 described in his thesis nine patterns found in fingerprints, but he also did not refer to the importance of fingerprints for recognition. Many authors thus began to use the prints of the palms of the hands and fingertips in personal signaling. However, the first who sensed that it was advantageous to use fingerprints to identify the offender was Henry Faulds since, as he himself wrote to the English magazine "Nature", if fingerprints are found at the crime scene, this can lead discovering the culprit. Subsequently in the late 1800s, Francis Galton and Edward Henry invented a relatively simple classification system, which divided the designs of the ridges and furrows into general types and subtypes. Galton, whose main interest was the use of fingerprints as an aid in the study of racial inheritance, published in 1892 a book, entitled "Fingerprints" in which he introduced the notion of minutia and suggested the first simple system of classification of fingerprints, based on grouping patterns into arches, loops and whorls. Galton soon discovered that fingerprints were of no use in determining the individual's genetic history, but scientifically proved their individuality and persistence. In 1891, Juan Vucetich, an Argentine police officer collected the first fingerprint files based on the classification of Galton, and in 1892 he made the first identification of a criminal by means of fingerprints. The Vucetich classification system is still in use in many Spanish-speaking countries. In England and Wales, the introduction of fingerprints for the identification of criminals began in 1901, based on the theories of Francis Galton later revised by Edward Richard Henry (who later became the chief commissioner of the London Metropolitan Police). The Galton-Henry classification system was published in June 1900, and adopted by numerous police offices in several states, and is still in use in all English-speaking countries. The first case of systematic application of fingerprints to identify people in the United States occurred in 1902 in the New York Civil Service Commission. Giovanni Gasti, an Italian too often forgotten, in 1905 further perfected the fingerprint classification system of Galton and Henry. Thus dactyloscopy was born.

Chapter five
"Serial killer and criminal profiling"

"It's said that everything is connected to everything.
The Butterfly Effect.
You drop a pebble into a pond, and the ripples radiate outwards,
touching and affecting everything.
Until finally a fish grows arms and legs and crawls out of the water.
And picks up a rock and smashes the next two fish over the head.
And we have the first serial killer.
MICHAEL C. HALL

According to the commonly accepted custom, the term "serial killer" was first used by Robert Ressler, FBI special agent, as well as one of the founding members of the Quantico-based Behavioral Sciences Unit (BSU), in Virginia. In the early 1970s Ressler, during a conference held at the British police academy, had heard some participants speak of "serial crime". In fact, this terminology meant a series of rapes, murders, thefts or arson attacks committed by the same person. Particularly impressed by this, on his return to Quantico Agent Ressler had started using the expression "serial killer", in order to describe "the crime of one who commits a murder, then another and another in a quite repetitive way ".

However, there would be some evidence that would testify to the existence and actual use of the term even before Ressler's alleged invention. Indeed, it would appear that the expression "serial killer" was explained in an edition prior to 1961 of the Merriam-Webster's Third New International Dictionary. Add to this that, in the book *The Meaning of Murder* by the British writer John Brophy, the word "serial murderer" is read several times. It would seem, therefore, that Robert Ressler may have drawn inspiration from Brophy. Beyond those who actually hold the credits for the invention of "serial killers", the large contribution made by Robert Ressler in the criminological field is undeniable. In 1979, together with Douglas, Burgess and Hartmann - other illustrious members of the BSU - he elaborated a classification of the murders on the basis of the victims, the style of killing adopted and the typology of the crime itself. Based on this classification, a distinction is made between mass murderer, spree killer and serial killer.

By Mass Murderer is meant the one who kills three or more people, through murders carried out in a single period of time and in the same place. These acts are often called "human time bomb" in jargon, as the killer, following a period characterized by several ruinous episodes, explodes, discharging his devastating violence against anyone in his range. So the killer generally doesn't know his victims. The Spree Killer is the one who kills two or more victims, in a short space of time and in different places. The triggering cause is often so unambiguous that the various murders are also linked together. However, the killer does not know his victims and the choice of target seems to be random. Finally, with the term Serial Killer, the FBI agents wanted to refer to the one who kills three or more victims in different places. The peculiarity is that this type of killer commits the murders following a cooling-off time between one kill and another. In addition, it is possible that he will kill even more people at a time. As for the choice of the victims, however, it can be either completely planned or random.

In later times, other important criminology exponents have provided different definitions of serial killers. In 1984, Egger highlighted the six main features of the serial killer:

1. commits at least two murders;

2. does not know the victim;

3. commits the murders at different times, without there being any correlation between one crime and another;

4. often commits murders in different places;

5. generally, he commits the murders in an impulsive way, without wanting to obtain a material gain, or he commits them with the aim of obtaining the gratification of some needs that he previously developed on an imaginative level;

6. the victims have similarities to each other.

In 1992 Brian Lane identified six other different elements capable of characterizing a serial murder:

#1. the murders are repeated at intervals (short or long) and can continue for years, until the killer is caught or dies of natural causes or commits suicide;

#2. the choice of the victim is generally random, although it can happen - albeit rarely - that the killer knows his victim;

#3. in most cases, there is no rational or well-defined motive, even if the victims may have traits in common and it seems that the killer has followed a specific pattern;

#4. the relationship between killer and victim turns out to be one-on-one, as is the case in individual killings;

#5. generally, murders are characterized by so-called overkilling, that is, a disproportionate use of violence on the victim's body, not aimed at carrying out the crime;

#6. there is great mobility from one place to another, thanks to the use of the car. Therefore, the killer can commit another murder before the previous one is discovered.

In Italy, Ruben De Luca (1998) reformulated the definition of serial killer formulated by the special agents of Quantico's behavioral sciences unit.

According to the author, a serial killer can be defined as one who personally commits two or more separate murders or exercises a psychological influence so that another person commits them in his place. De Luca highlighted that in order to speak of a serial murderer, there must be a clear intention to repeatedly kill, even if the victims survive or the crimes are not carried out. Generally, the serial killer acts alone, but it is not excluded that he can act as part of a couple or within a larger group, playing the role of leader. Also in Italy, Mastronardi (2008) studied 2228 serial killers worldwide. Thanks to intense research, he traced a profile of the serial killer, focusing on male individuals:

1. the first murder is committed between 20 and 30 years of age;

2. during adolescence, frequently manifests violent behavior;

3. does not know his victims;

4. the victims are generally women;

5. exercises dominion by making the victim impotent;

6. presents problems at work level;

7. in the evolutionary period, shows little or no interest in sexual activity;

8. prefers weapons that allow him to have physical contact with the victim (ropes, knives, etc.)

9. shows interest in investigations;

10. about four years pass before he is caught;

11. frequent predatory attitude;

12. moves easily.

The stages of serial murder

Through a series of interviews with serial killers, the penitentiary psychologist Joel Norris (1988) analyzed the various phases that make up a serial murder. In particular, it showed the differentiation of the pre-predatory, predatory and post-predatory activity. Based on this, he identified seven phases: aura phase, trolling, wooing, capture, murder, totem phase and depression phase. In the first phase, the killer experiences a series of essentially peculiar phenomena. He perceives a slowness in the passage of time, a greater vividness of sounds and colors and a more intense sensitivity of the skin. During this period, he begins to imagine his homicidal project. The aura phase can last a few minutes or a few months. The trolling phase is the moment of the victim's unstoppable search. In this sense, the killer carefully chooses the places to wait and identify the target. After choosing the victim, he follows her to study her usual movements. Next, there is the wooing stage. The subject finally begins to implement his plan. First, he approaches the victim, using a polite or seductive attitude, trying not to insinuate doubts or terrorize her, so as to gain her trust. The capture phase can be understood as the second step of predatory activity, in which the killer captures the victim. This can happen suddenly or gradually. Generally, the event occurs in an isolated place, because the killer needs to exercise his dominance over the victim, undisturbed and using the time he needs. In the murder phase, the crime is actually carried out. The killer experiences the maximum level of excitement when he kills the victim. Some individuals may even reach orgasm. All this is accompanied by a feeling of triumph. Penultimate, the totem phase, in which the feelings of triumph and excitement begin to gradually disappear. Therefore, the killer preserves the victim's body or part of it or subtracts some objects, in order to keep the memory of the murder and prolong the pleasure. Finally, there is the depressive phase. The killer understands that the murder and the triumph associated with it did not change his past, but it was only a passing sensation. Therefore, he enters a depressive phase, even if, with the passage of time, he will return to fantasizing about the murder; in this way, the cycle will start again.

From criminal profiling to classifications of serial killers

Law enforcement agencies manage to identify a serial killer through a process called "criminal profiling". It consists of a set of psychological techniques that allow to trace a profile of the alleged perpetrator of the crime, through the study of the nature of the crime and the ways in which it was committed. In this regard, Holmes and Holmes (1996) noted the three objectives that criminal profiling has: psychological and social evaluation of the killer, psychological evaluation of the findings that the suspect has stolen from the victim, advice to investigators on the most appropriate interrogation techniques. In this sense, the psychological profile assumes some characteristics of the alleged offender: age, sex, ethnicity, marital status/adaptation to the relationship, socio-economic status, residence, characteristics of the means of transport used, IQ, school and work achievements, lifestyle, self-care, educational environment of origin, sexual sphere and possible perversions, motive, previous contacts with justice and/or mental health services, personality characteristics. However, Pinizzotto and Finkel (1990) have highlighted how the identification of the suspect and therefore his psychological profile cannot be separated from the knowledge of two elements: what happened and why it happened. For the authors, "what happened" can be detected by analyzing the crime scene, the medical-legal relationship and the modus operandi. In short, the modus operandi is the behavior that the killer has put in place to carry out the crime. "Why it happened" can be investigated by looking for the motive and the signature. Thanks to the birth and development of this set of techniques, it appeared necessary to make classifications capable of distinguishing and identifying the psychological profile of the killer. Among the main classifications proposed, we mention that made by two US psychiatrists, Dietz and Rappaport.

In 1986, they highlighted the presence of five types of serial killers:

a) Crime Spree Killers: individuals whose murders are connected with other crimes (theft, drug trafficking, robbery...). They can act alone, in pairs or within a group.

b) Functionaries of Organized Criminal Operations: often associated with organized crime (e.g., international drug trafficking cartels), they commit murders on commission or to obtain a personal advantage.

c) Custodial Poisoners and Asphyxiators: generally, they work in the health sector and kill patients to obtain economic benefits or with the aim of "relieving" them from their illness and from being dependent on other people.

d) Psychotics: this category includes those who kill because they are moved by irrational thoughts, such as hearing voices that push them to commit such acts or believe they are acting because they are commanded by God.

e) Sexual Sadists: they use sex to inflict further pain on the victim, who is tortured before being killed.

The classification of Ressler, Burges and Douglas (1988) is different. The three BSU agents made a profound distinction between disorganized serial killer and organized serial killer. This is a classification still particularly used today especially in the investigation field, as it allows investigators to grasp, in the crime scene, important details useful for the delineation of the criminal profile. The organized serial killer carefully chooses the victims, according to specific physical characteristics, and carefully plans the entire murder process. Instead, the disorganized serial killer tends to act suddenly and impulsively. For this reason, the victims are chosen completely randomly, and the killer could leave traces in the crime scene. One scholar in particular, Newton (1990), has created a classification based on the mobility, displacements and range of action of serial killers, distinguishing between territorial serial killers, nomadic serial killers and stationary serial killers. With "Territorial Serial Killer" the author intended the individual who commits the murders within a well-established range of action. The "Nomadic Serial Killer" is someone who seeks the ideal victim by moving from one place to another. Finally, the "Stationary Serial Killer" is intended as the person whose crimes are committed within his home or workplace.

We also remember the work of Stephen and Ronald Holmes, who were among the main advisors of the FBI. In addition to defining the serial killer as a "predator that kills three or more people in a span of more than a month", they have proposed a classification in which each typology is distinguished on the basis of the victim's choice process, the way where the murder is carried out and the places where the crimes are committed. The four types of serial killers are: Visionary Serial Killer, Missionary Serial Killer,

Hedonistic Serial Killer, Control and Power Oriented Serial Killer. The Visionary Serial Killer is an individual who suffers from a serious detachment from reality, experienced through the fact of "hearing voices" and/or having visions. He commits murders because he believes he is another person or has been forced to kill a person by the devil, by God or by angels. He does not have an ideal type of victim: he chooses the target randomly. Often, the victim lives in the same area of action as the killer, who takes advantage of the opportunity to act on the ground he knows and where he feels comfortable. Since the victim is chosen randomly, there is no pre-predatory selection and activity process. The murder occurs quickly and the killer acts as if he should complete a task. Given the absence of planning of the act, he can use a weapon found at the crime scene. The Missionary Serial Killer consciously decides to take the lives of some types of people, as he believes that they must necessarily be killed, as in a mission. So, the victims are generally prostitutes, clochards, homosexuals, drug dealers. He does not derive economic or material advantages from the commission of a crime, but psychological advantages. The pre-predatory phase is in fact characterized by an extensive activity related to the killer's fantasies. The act occurs quickly, but with considerable planning, which allows the killer to leave few traces on the crime scene. Instead, the Hedonistic Serial Killer is the one who experiences a state of pleasure the moment he kills. For this reason, a distinction is made between:

• hedonistic serial killer oriented towards the search for sexual pleasure, in which the essential motivation is sex linked to an intense violent sexual fantasy;

• hedonistic serial killer oriented towards the thrill, in which this "thrill" is experienced through a series of sadistic acts inflicted on the victim;

• hedonistic serial killer oriented to the search for personal gain, in which the murder allows him to obtain economic gains and/or other material profits.

The fourth type, the Control and Power Oriented Serial Killer, characterizes the one who derives pleasure from the possibility of dominating the victim and from the fact that the victim's life depends on him. Power is therefore exercised through psychological manipulation or physical force. The victim is selected based on some physical characteristics, even if the killer does not know her. Furthermore, due to the need to enjoy from the state of submission of the target, the murder does not take place immediately, but after a certain period of time.

However, in 1995, the American psychiatrist David Lester proposed a particularly innovative differentiation. Moving away from the classifications made by other scholars in the field, he focused on the distinction between:

1. serial killer among Nazi criminals;

2. organized crime serial killer;

3. terrorists;

4. serial killers in youth gangs;

5. pirates and outlaws of the old American West.

Particularly noteworthy is the complex classification proposed by Ruben De Luca and Vincenzo Maria Mastronardi in 2005. The two Italian experts have in fact identified ten types of serial killers. First, they divided the killers into two main categories: "Classic Serial Killer" and "Anomalous Serial Killer". The Classic Serial Killer is the type most present in the news. By this expression is meant the "classic" killer, who captures the victim and kills her, perpetrating perpetrating an act of sexual violence or not. Generally, this individual kills victims through ways that allow him to maintain physical contact with the target, as this increases his sense of pleasure. In a characteristic way, he follows the seven phases of the homicidal activity hypothesized by Norris and tends to take trophies or fetishes from the victim's corpse; these objects allow him to relive the murder and increase the pleasure. Furthermore, he does not kill for material advantages or driven by jealousy or revenge, but to satisfy his internal psychological need. In the macro category of Anomalous Serial Killer, all killers who do not fall into the category mentioned above are included. For example, we are faced with Anomalous Serial Killer in the case of murders with a mafia matrix, terrorist murders with characteristics of sadism or even ritual murders. However, De Luca and Mastronardi have distinguished, within this macro category, three types of Serial Killer, which differ from each other based on the execution mode: Arsonist Serial Killer, Bomber Serial Killer and Sniper Serial Killer. The Arsonist Serial Killer acts with the intent of destroying and killing, but he also wants to maintain control of the crime scene from an external position. For these reasons, he acts in places where he is sure to find many people. This differentiates him from the arsonist, who sets fires for the sole sake of doing it and without having the intention of killing someone. The Bomber Serial Killer also controls the crime scene from the outside and acts in order to have no physical contact with the victim.

This type of serial killer is divided into two other sub-categories: the "unabomber model" killer, which builds bombs aimed at killing one person at a time; the "slaughter model" killer, whose dynamite action is designed to assassinate multiple victims at the same time. The essential feature of the Sniper Serial Killer is randomness. This individual tends to lurk in a hidden place, holding a sniper rifle. Then he shoots a victim, whose choice depends solely on whether he was in that place and at that time. As De Luca has defined, it is a sort of "target shooting" game and the killer is particularly difficult to identify, both for the absence of relationship between him and the victim and for his absence in the scene of crime. Within their classification, De Luca and Mastronardi have demonstrated the existence of four types of serial killers, distinct from the method by which the victims are chosen. The "Would-be Serial Killer" is hardly recognizable.

They are those who are arrested after only one murder, but who, thanks to an analysis of the motive, certainly had the intention of committing other murders. Generally, these are cases in which the individual is arrested, serves his sentence in prison and, once he has regained his freedom, commits other murders having the same characteristics as the first. The Serial Killer for Fun is the one who kills for a playful purpose. In fact, he kills because of boredom and to seek strong emotions, which he cannot experience otherwise. With Mass Serial Killer, the authors refer to those who repeat the murder action over time, killing multiple victims at the same time. Often, victims are chosen randomly and in short intervals of time, as if it were a single massacre. It's also possible that mass serial killers don't bother about hiding their tracks and getting caught. The Ritual Serial Killer commits murders according to rituals rigidly determined by the culture of belonging. According to this, the crime is carried out through a rigid and predefined scheme. The last category highlighted by the two Italian authors is the Serial Killer by Proxy. These are cases in which it is not the subject itself who performs the murder, but acts to ensure that other people do it in his place. For this reason, he is generally adept at exercising a certain mental power over others. However, the responsibility related to the crime is equally divided between those who induce to kill and those who execute it materially.

The behavior of Serial Killers in the crime scene

When we talk about the behaviors or execution methods used by serial killers within the crime scene, the modus operandi and the signature immediately come to mind. Although usually we tend to consider them as two identical concepts and as if they were synonymous with each other, in reality they differ considerably. Nevertheless, it is not excluded that there are cases in which they can coincide. The term modus operandi (MO) refers to the execution methods or behavior used by the serial killer to implement the murder plan. It is clarified that it is a dynamic behavior and that it may undergo variations over time and crimes.

In fact, it can be modified by the killer himself for two main reasons. The first refers to the possibility of reducing the risk of being identified and subsequently captured. The second concerns the need to optimize the gratification deriving from the murder. According to Carmelo Lavorino (2000), the modus operandi of a serial killer can be defined as a "Chronological Organizational Matrix of the Murder", commonly called with the acronym COMM.

COMM is made up of a process that can be divided into eight phases:

1. decision-making phase, in which the killer reaches the decision to kill one or more people, while imagining the consequences that will inevitably arise from this act;

2. organizational-planning phase, the moment in which the offender plans how the murder will take place;

3. victim predisposition phase, in which the target is chosen and its characteristics are analyzed;

4. phase of preparation of the crime scene, in which the places where the crime will be physically committed are chosen;

5. execution phase, the moment in which the previously chosen

victim is actually captured and killed;

6. overkilling and after killing phase, characterized by that set of behaviors implemented, after the death of the target, in an aggressive and exaggerated way compared to the amount of force necessary to kill the victim;

7. stage alteration and self-cover phase, during which the killer manipulates the crime scene, with the aim of eliminating all traces of himself;

8. phase of distancing from murder, the last phase, in which the offender leaves the crime scene and returns to the usual activities.

It is useful to analyze the modus operandi, since it provides indications about the presence of possible linkages between one murder case and the other. Furthermore, in serial killers, the modus operandi can be essentially based on an aggressive approach or on a seductive approach. The aggressive approach generally outlines killers who have poor verbal and social skills, experience feelings of inadequacy or feel tense during interactions. Therefore, they tend to capture the victim using coercion and physical constraint. On the contrary, the seductive approach is typical of those who demonstrate a broad confidence in their skills and are socially able, thanks to their charismatic qualities. These individuals begin to anticipate the moment of killing during the interaction with the chosen victim. To achieve their goal, they convince the targets to follow them, always using kind ways. The signature is, instead, a behavior carried out by the serial killer, according to a ritual and static modality, and which is not necessary for carrying out the criminal act itself. In fact, it identifies the behavior of a particular individual and tends to repeat itself in all - or almost all - of his crime scenes. Douglas and his associates in 2008 determined that the signature reflects the personalization of the crime. Indeed, Mastronardi and De Luca spoke of "a kind of business card of the person who acts". Precisely for these reasons, unlike the modus operandi, the signature is static, does not vary over time, but rather tends to always appear in the same way. In addition, it constitutes a sort of ritual used repeatedly by the person who committed the crime. The signature does not necessarily occur in all crime scenes; however, when detected, it reflects the deep fantasies and dynamics that led the subject to perform the heinous gesture. To understand how the signature can be distinguished from the modus operandi, the way in which the killer handles the victim's body after the murder can be taken into consideration. We will talk about modus operandi if the disposition of the corpse performs a purely instrumental function, that is to facilitate the killer. For example, the victim could be hidden to delay the investigation and the consequent capture of the murderer. Instead, it will be a part of the signature if the victim's body performs the expressive function of sending a particular message. In this case, the serial killer could abandon the corpse in a certain place or position with the intent of expressing his profound contempt for the victim. However, there are also other types of executive modalities that can be used in the crime scene. First of all, staging. It is nothing more than the deliberate alteration of the crime scene, carried out before abandoning it and before the intervention of the police.

This alteration can be practiced, in the first place, with the intent of sidetracking the investigations and diverting investigators from the possible motive. At the same time, it can be used to protect the victim or the victim's family. A particular form of staging is called undoing, a term that indicates the deliberate alteration of the crime scene with the aim of appeasing one's remorse for the act and putting some remedy. For example, the serial killer can cleanse the corpse of blood, cover it or position it in a non-degrading way. Usually, this modification is implemented when there is a close relationship between the killer and his victim and, above all, when the victim represents a significant figure for the offender. Two other behaviors that the murderer can employ consist of personation and mutilation.

By personation is meant behavior that is of no use in completing the murder. In this case, the crime scene has an intimate and profound meaning that only the serial killer is aware of. This definition includes behaviors such as mutilating parts of the body, remove or insert objects at the crime scene (especially in the genitals or near the corpse), position the victim in specific ways (for example, so that he remembers a certain religious symbol). However, everything must have a meaning. Mutilation is the removal of a part of the victim's body. Generally, it is the removal of a limb, or part of it, or the genitals. Mutilation can have a defensive, aggressive, offensive or necromatic purpose. It is defensive when the motivation for the gesture lies in concealing or moving the corpse more easily. In this sense, the body can also be dismembered, so that it is less recognizable. Aggressive mutilation represents the culmination of the outburst of strong anger towards the victim. Mutilation is offensive when it has an exclusively lustful meaning.

In conclusion, the reason that drives the offender to mutilate according to a necromatic purpose lies in the possibility of using the removed area as a trophy.

Special Content: The story of Harvey Glatman, the photographer serial killer

We are in Los Angeles in the late 1950s, precisely between 1957 and 1958. A toolbox is found in Harvey Glatman's apartment. When opened, horror is discovered: photos depicting women with their hands tied behind their backs, terror painted on their faces. In an orderly manner, other photos were arranged, the subjects of which are the same as the others but, in this case, they are dead. Thus began the investigations against Glatman. It turns out that he grew up in Colorado. As a child, he was quite frail, lonely and a victim of bullies because of his "bunny teeth". During adolescence, he begins to exhibit strange sexual tendencies. Around the age of 12, the mother opens the door of his room and finds him intent on suffocating himself with a rope, for pure sexual pleasure. But his weirdness doesn't end there. Harvey enters the women's apartments, then ties them up, rapes them and photographs them. His tendencies stop for a while, when, in 1945, he is captured while trying to break into a home. However, he is released on bail. Subsequently, he rapes a woman and is then sentenced to eight months in prison. Months pass, Harvey Glatman regains his freedom and moves to Albany, in the state of New York. Here, he returns to prison due to some robberies and is diagnosed with psychopathy. But Harvey proves to be particularly respectful of the rules and in 1951 he is released on parole.

In 1957, he decides to change cities again and start over with a new life. He moves to Los Angeles and uses several pseudonyms, pretending to be a photographer.

In fact, his intent is to entice beautiful and young women, promising them a modeling career. Since his victims must respect certain physical characteristics, he looks for them directly in the model agencies. After expertly baiting them, he lures them into hotel rooms, where he offers them money but on one condition: they have to take bondage positions. However, he reassures them by saying that those photos will be published in some police magazines. His first victim is 19-year-old Judy Ann Dull, who was experiencing a period of economic hardship at the time, given her recent separation from her husband. Harvey offers her $ 50 to pose and the girl accepts. Once they arrive in the hotel room, however, everything changes. He points a gun at her face, ties her and rapes her violently. In the meantime, he takes some photos. Then he strangles her and photographs her again and finally leaves the body of the 19 year old in the Mojavi desert, just outside Los Angeles. The second victim is a 24-year-old model named Shirley Ann Bridgeford.

The victim had just come out of a divorce, and knew her future killer through an announcement for lonely hearts that he had left by signing up with the name of George Williams. He is very kind and invites her to a dance; she accepts. They will never get to the ball. He brings her home, binds her, rapes her and photographs her; later, he kills her and photographs her again, only to abandon her in the desert. 24-year-old model Ruth Mercado is the third victim. The two know each other through an announcement for lonely hearts. Harvey asks her to pose for him, but as usual he ties her up, rapes her repeatedly while taking some photos. She is killed, photographed and abandoned in the same desert. "I made them kneel. I did the same thing with each of them. With the gun pointed, I tied them with a little rope to their ankles, then to the neck and hands. Finally, I stayed there waiting until they stopped fussing", the serial killer will tell during the trial. October 27, 1958. Harvey had contacted a girl a few days earlier through a modeling agency. Her name is Lorraine Vigil and she is 28 years old. The model agrees to get in the car with him, but as soon as she sees that he is driving in the opposite direction to Hollywood, she becomes alarmed. A few hours later, she will declare to the agents: "I was not worried until we entered the Santa Ana highway. Here he started going at tremendous speed and he wasn't answering my questions". And in fact Lorraine gets so upset that, at one point,

Harvey points the gun at her head and tries to tie her up. An agent assists the entire scene and intervenes immediately. Harvey Glatman is arrested and confesses to the three murders. Then, he shows the police his toolbox in which all the photographs of the victims are found. He is found guilty on two counts of first degree murder and sentenced to death. The gas chamber of San Quentin prison kills him on September 18, 1959.

Chapter Six
"Criminal profiling and sex offenders"

"Slums may well be breeding grounds of crime,
but middle class suburbs are
incubators of apathy and delirium".

PALINURUS

Sexual murder involves a sexual element underlying a sequence of facts that lead to death. The implementation and meaning of this sexual element varies according to the offender. The action can vary from actual rape that includes penetration (both pre and postmortem), to a symbolic sexual assault, such as the insertion of foreign bodies into the victim's orifices. The sexual act is the basis of facts that lead to death. The difference between a sexually motivated murder and another is the offender's action: an effective rape or a symbolic sexual assault. By organized offender we mean an individual who appears to plan his murders, selects his victims and shows great control over the crime scene. A methodical and orderly approach is manifested during all phases of the crime.

The victim is usually female, of the same race as the offender, single, works and lives alone. Male teenagers are also targeted. The risk factor is determined by the victim's lifestyle, what she does in life and her physical traits. Prostitutes or hitchhikers, for example, victims that the offender knows where to find. The elderly and young people can be victims because they have a lower degree of defense. The danger to the victim is greater if the attack occurs in isolated areas, or if it occurs at night. It is usually an occasional victim that the attacker does not know, and which responds to certain personal canons. The victims share common characteristics such as age, physical appearance, occupation, hairstyle or lifestyle. An overly confident or careless mental attitude towards personal safety can raise an individual's chances of becoming a victim. The offender is often a socially skilled individual that uses manipulation to entice the victim. He may have had a pseudo relationship as a prelude to aggression. The killer may play another role, such as that of a police officer or security guard, a person in uniform, to gain the victim's trust; he often returns to check some or all of the crime scenes (the places of the kidnapping, the attack or the place where the body is buried). He can also take part in the investigation cooperatively or by providing false information.

This attitude has two main purposes: to check the state of the investigation and relive the crime. What is his past? Events that may have caused severe stress such as: financial or work problems, or marital problems or concerning any type of relationship etc. He may have recently changed residence or jobs. He acts on impulse because of the stress, so the victim could live in the vicinity of the attacker, who draws security from the familiar environments that reinforce his feelings of social inadequacy. The victims may not have similar characteristics in common. An individual typically becomes a victim of chance, since she is in the wrong place at the wrong time. The other considerations regarding the estimate of the risk taken by the victim or offender are the same as those of the classification "Murder of a sexual - organized nature". The disorganized offender is generally socially inept, and has a strong sense of inadequacy. These feelings of deficiency push him to attack the victim by surprise, trying to immobilize her immediately. The injuries inflicted in a disorganized sex murder are caused when the offender feels more comfortable and less intimidated by the victim. Sexual injuries and assaults occur when the victim is unconscious, about to die, or after death. Signs of depersonalization, such as mutilation of part of the face and overkill (an excessive amount or severity of wounds) on certain parts of the body. The parts most often targeted are the face, breasts and genitals. Parts of the body may also be missing from the scene. The offender could also use ropes and coercion tools. Post mortem sexual acts such as insertion of foreign objects into the body's orifices (insertion necrophilia). Traces of seminal fluid can be found on the victim's clothing or, less frequently, on the wounds, since there is almost never the actual act of penetration. The disorganized offender usually lives alone or with a parental figure. He lives or works near the crime scene. He has a past of work and relationship failures. The disorganized sex offender is considered a little strange by those who know him, with unusual habits; usually following the murder he could show interest by asking several questions about the incident, and could increase the consumption of alcohol. There may be multiple offenders involved, therefore with different behavior patterns; the aggression can begin in an orderly and planned way, but become disorganized due to an unexpected event (victim difficult to control, someone else's arrival at the crime scene or stressors that he cannot manage). He derives sexual excitement from his own fantasies.

Sexual gratification is achieved by inflicting pain on the victim through physical and mental torture methods. The more the victim suffers, the more he gets pleasure. Sadistic sexual fantasies are persistent and aim to dominate the victim, inflicting extreme violence to the point of death. The victimology of this crime tends to refer to female victims but can also include men and children. Usually a central role is given by the similarity of the victim with an important reference figure of the sexual sadistic offender. Usually he approaches the victim after stalking, with an empathic attitude and usually asking for information. The victim does not realize the danger because the offender's attitude and behavior is affable and extremely friendly. Because of his sexual fantasies, the sadistic sex offender has to spend a lot of time with the victim because the excitement comes from the pain the victim feels, and usually the place where the torture takes place is a secluded place. There are usually three crime scenes: the place of enticement, the place of torture and the place where the corpse is released. The sadistic sex offender prepares carefully for the choice of the victim and for torture, and he is very careful not to leave fingerprints. There are usually traces of overkill and depersonalization to hide the victim's identity. He can carry out staging activities to conceal the murder and to suggest that a different crime has occurred. Sexual assault can take place by inserting foreign objects into the victim's sexual cavities. The act of killing is often eroticized; death comes in a slow and deliberate way that the offender tastes slowly. Often the offender makes the victim pass out and revives her immediately afterwards. The most common cause of death is asphyxiation caused by strangulation with the use of ropes, manual strangulation, hanging and suffocation. These offenders are mainly male; sometimes the presence of an accomplice, a man or a woman, can be detected.

The offender often has a job that connects him to the public. He demonstrates antisocial behavior that often leads to frequent arrests. The offender can return to the crime scene to determine if the body has been found or to monitor the progress made by the investigation. Antisocial personality disorder alongside other very serious personality and sexual disorders, such as narcissistic disorder and sadism, characterize the psychopathology of the serial killer.

Special content: Serial Killer: 12 warning signs

Without generalizing and without formulating hypotheses of direct causality, the twelve most common characteristics of a serial killer are analyzed below.

1. Social isolation. Strong feelings of isolation during childhood. These are children in whom fantasy takes on a predominant role and compensates for a reality poor in positive stimuli. These fantasies have the characteristic of being prematurely sexualized with contents that deeply disturb the child, but, at the same time, excite him. The child is seduced by his fantasy world, which is not a fairy tale one, and progressively moves away from the real world;

2. Learning difficulties. Physical and mental damage, early deprivation and a chronic lack of confidence around him are all factors that contribute to creating school failure, a situation common to many serial killers. Although most of them have an average or even high IQ, they cannot bear the weight of their studies, due to the same internal anxiety that causes their inconstancy in the work field;

3. Symptoms of neurological damage. This damage can be caused by an injury or illness. In some cases, severe head trauma is associated with the sudden appearance of aggressive behavior and/or excessive personality;

4. Irregular behavior. It is characterized above all by an unmotivated and chronic need to lie, hypochondria and chameleon-like behavior, used to mask social deviance. As children, many serial killers begin to lie compulsively, because this activity gives them a strong excitement and a feeling of power;

5. Problems with the authorities and self-control. Often, the child suffers when parents entrust him to other relatives or strangers and when school teachers change too frequently. They are children unable to tolerate restrictions and who react extremely to the slightest frustration;

6. Early viewing of pornographic material. Many times, serial killers start masturbating as children or demonstrate violent and abusive sexuality towards others. The use of pornographic material also begins at an early age. In particular, serial killers make abundant use of pornography, although it is not possible to establish a direct correlation between the two behaviors.

7. Early and bizarre sexual activity. As children, serial killers are often forced to have sexual experiences, as they are victims of both intra and extra-family violence. This leads them to a form of attraction-repulsion for sex, which begins to become an obsessive thought in their mind;

8. Obsession with fire, blood and death. Serial killers, as children, are often obsessed with destructive fantasies that sometimes lead to real arson that goes beyond the normal games with matches made by all children. For the child or teenager serial killer, starting a fire satisfies two very strong drives: the first is destructive, common to all children, the second is sexual. When this type of behavior arises in childhood, it means that the subject feels deeply inadequate, therefore rebels by destroying objects. For the teenager serial killer, pyromania is a means of releasing their sexual tensions. Serial killers also pay particular attention to blood during their evolutionary period. For some of them, this is related to a real physical need to have blood contact. Another obsession frequently encountered in the evolutionary period of many serial killers is that of death. These subjects, instead of feeling a natural repulsion towards everything related to death, are fascinated by it, so that some authors speak of "necromania";

9. Cruelty to animals and / or other people. Experts who study the phenomenon advise never to underestimate the violent games of children towards animals, because these behaviors can be signs of unease that can herald the development of a violent personality;

10. Theft and hoarding disorder. They are symptoms of the child's emotional void. Theft is often the first step in the serial killer's criminal career. This behavior can appear at a very early age and then lead to real armed robberies over time. Sometimes, theft is connected to deviations from the sexual sphere such as voyeurism and fetishism;

11. Self-destructive behavior. The "self-mutilation syndrome" can last for decades in which self-mutilation alternates with moments of absolute calm and impulsive behaviors, such as eating disorders, alcohol and other substance abuse and kleptomania. In the F.B.I. sample, 19% said they had practiced self-mutilation during childhood;

12. Early drug abuse. It is a way of psychic escape from reality or of emulation of parental behavior and is very common among serial killers. Most of the time the parents themselves, and in particular the father, provide the model to the child. Often the killers who start killing when they are still teenagers make frequent use of these substances, to give themselves courage and look like "real men".

Chapter Seven
"Criminology and sectarian drift"

"There are among the people murderers who have never committed murder, hieves who have never stolen and liars who have spoken nothing but the truth".
KAHLIL GIBRAN

We are what we have. It is television, newspapers, cinema and the internet that decide who we should be, who will be successful and who will not. We can be successful people only if we comply with their dictates, only if we follow their rules, only if we buy their products. That product is absolutely necessary because it is fashionable. Regardless of what we need, we need to buy it right away. We are no longer able to recognize our real needs. Affective, emotional, relational needs. The need to get bored, to waste time, to sleep. The need to listen to us, to be with ourselves. It is a continuous race. We live in a society that forces us to success, to fame, and tells us that whoever stops is lost. But why? This frantic race to get us always different and increasingly intense experiences creates a sort of emotional anesthesia. We are no longer able to get excited about simple things, to enjoy them, to appreciate what is different, to feel curiosity, to want to discover new things. We lose the ability to critically evaluate what surrounds us. Television and the internet are our means of contact with the world, and they tell us stories of life and exasperated, harsh, raw and violent images, which, however, do not affect us much. Who is shocked to hear about death and war? The news now bores us.

We experience real emotional anesthesia, and empathy also becomes difficult. Humanity is in crisis, it is nothing new. Culture, institutions, thinking, values, projects, roles, identities are in crisis. We are what we produce. Everything today is directly connected to money. We acquire value as people if we produce a lot and in a short time. Those who are unable to produce are worthless, it is no coincidence that we continually forget the needs and existence of elderly or disabled people. They don't produce, they don't work, they don't serve, they don't have value, and yet they exist. Social ties are in crisis. Teens manage to establish relationships only if mediated by the use of mobile phones and computers. Sometimes they also talk to their parents via messages, and parents have adapted to this system. Face-to-face relationships have become difficult, they are tiring.

The family is changing, nuclear families (married couple and any legitimate children) are less and less frequent and single-parent or reconstituted families are more and more frequent. The rate of separations and divorces is steadily increasing. We live in the era of communication, but we find it increasingly difficult to have stable, serene and sincere relationships. Affective relationships enter into crisis when the first phase of falling in love ends, and the other person becomes a source of anxiety and fear. Fear of losing your identity, your goals, your projects. Fear of getting lost. This anxiety and fear in emotional relationships have their origin in the narcissism towards which we are driven by the context in which we live: self-affirmation at all costs, success at all costs, attention to oneself and one's needs, the alienation and depersonalization of the other. The search for the meaning of life is increasingly entrusted to the individual. Individualism. Attention to oneself has put in crisis values such as that of trust, solidarity and reciprocity. We need others, but we don't know how much. Experiencing strong emotions reminds us that we are alive, therefore we are looking for increasingly intense and always different emotions to feel alive, happy. Here then is that "happiness" becomes the key word of the modern world, the emblem of modernity.

That's why the pursuit of happiness opens the door to a series of characters of dubious morality who promise and sell happiness to people. The insecurity, confusion and precariousness that modern man experiences pushes him to take on any bait in order to suddenly feel happy. Hundreds of pseudo-religious groups exploit this mood by bringing people closer to new cults, also promising them the much desired happiness. Of these, the most captivating are certainly the esoteric groups, which make use of magic, which man has always used to have control over external events and phenomena that he could not understand. The fascination of the occult therefore lies in the illusion of being able to directly influence one's condition, modifying it in relation to one's own needs, of having power over oneself and others rather than feeling at the mercy of external events. Sects, congregations and pseudo-religious associations find themselves in the right place and at the right time, in a fragmented society that generates equally fragmented and frightened individuals. These groups offer a vision of the world that is already widespread and known, to which they add new and different elements that can give a religious explanation to the unease and evil of society, without however straying too far from the majority culture. They appeal to a few followers and remain rather small groups; this is so that members can feel important, bind and intertwine faster, without feeling anonymous, abandoned and lost as in external society. Various studies have verified that the people who are interested and who end up joining a sect are people who have experienced a series of negative experiences on an individual level, such as problems during the primary socialization phase, periods of constant change , failures on a relational or work level. Joining a sect is a way to claim, not to give up, to try to react to your discomfort. Apparently it works, because a very strong mechanism of cohesion and socialization is generated within the sect. Finally we feel like someone, finally we feel part of something, finally we feel important. Being part of a sect increases self-esteem and decreases anxiety. You have the feeling that you can control any aspect of your life and thus put an end to your frustration.

Getting in is very easy, getting out is very difficult. Leaving a sect is difficult precisely for these reasons. Losing the support and references that have given meaning to one's being in the world, that have given importance and attention to one's own person, that have generated psychological and sometimes even physical well-being, is difficult for a fragile ego. The term "sect" can have two interpretations depending on the etymological root attributed to it. Sect can derive from the Latin *secta*, from the verb *secor*, which means "to follow, go behind", or it can also derive from the verb *seco*, which means "to cut, separate, disconnect". So if you adopt the first derivation a sect is a group of people who decide to follow a particular doctrine or leader. According to the second derivation, however, a sect is a group of people who have separated themselves from a majority doctrine.

The groups labeled as sects have always been groups of a religious nature, which have separated and opposed to official religions, have created new principles and new dogmas, adopting their own different vision of the world and their own lifestyle. It is a phenomenon that began to grow in the early 1900s, coinciding with the processes of schooling and secularization, whereby religious institutions began to lose credibility and social significance. In particular, in the 1960s and 1970s, youth movements started a process of globalization and rediscovery of spirituality. In this climate dozens of new sects and new religious movements have arisen, precisely to depart from the strict and unfulfilling conformism of previous years. In recent years, the term sect has been associated with a negative connotation, because religious groups have always frightened the majority since they have always been very closed to the outside and shrouded in mystery. Getting in is easy, it's a choice. We choose not to follow the official doctrine anymore to follow a minority that seems to respond better to our needs and our questions. Generally all sects have a hierarchical and pyramidal structure that sees a "charismatic leader" at the head, who is almost always the founder of the sect. Below him, depending on how the group has decided to organize itself, there may be celebrants, ministers, elder brothers and sisters, main members. The elder sisters and brothers have the task of instructing the recruiters, who in turn have the task of looking for new followers. The main members, on the other hand, tend to deal with the new followers. New adepts must always support a path of initiation and personal transformation which, in most cases, is not devoid of forms of psychological conditioning and mental manipulation.

Chapter Eighth
"Youth and sectarian drift"

"You can imagine my embarrassment when I killed the wrong guy."

JOE VALACHI

It is known that adolescence and rebellion are often synonymous. During adolescence, rebellion is a positive symptom of growth. Rejecting, reacting, challenging and rebelling against the adult world is necessary so that the young person can build his own identity and no longer be dependent on that of his parents. The whole adult world is rejected: the way of dressing, the way of speaking, the way of eating, the way of thinking. How many times do we see scenes in malls where a mother shows her daughter a shirt and she replies that it "sucks"? As soon as adolescence begins, teen start to say a lot of bad words, or they invent new ones that parents don't know. Reject the adult world, reject the limits within which the life of one's parents takes place, overcome them, scandalize them. Sex no longer scandalizes so much, and neither do drugs. But Satanism does. Young people who choose Satanism experience the exact same discomfort and the same identical frustration as all other teenagers, but they choose a doctrine that in reality has little to teach from an ethical, moral and religious point of view has little to teach. Still, Satanism has its charm because mysterious things always attract a little more. The occult fascinates, as does magic. The idea of being able to use magic makes one feel special, gives a sense of power and omnipotence. The teenager is also interested in Satanism because he has the opportunity to use drugs and make sex easy, without having to go look for it elsewhere. By using drugs, by being part of a group that is not well viewed by the outside world and by committing crimes, albeit minor ones (such as if he decides to steal money in order to buy drugs, or threats an outside person for favors), the young man does nothing but challenge authority, the system, society and adults. Why not choose Satanism? It promises power, control, success, it gives the idea of being invincible and special, which is basically everything towards which today's society pushes us. Be a successful person, have everything you want. It is difficult to be a teenager today: you have to challenge an adult world that is in crisis itself, that is a teenager itself. The young person, who would need to face a solid cultural system, finds instability, emptiness and fragmentation. While in the past young people clashed with a solid social world, and from the conflict with it they could build an adult identity with equally strong values and roles, today this is no longer possible, and teenagers struggle to understand the world from which they must separate, bombarded with alexithymic media messages. We are what we have. You only have value if you are successful. The teenagers most at risk are those who have a conflictual relationship with their parents, the lonely, the poorly communicative, who do not feel accepted by the peer group or have difficulty socializing, who have low self-esteem, who are particularly insecure. For them, Satanism becomes the ideal solution to overcome the feelings of inadequacy and weakness. Cantelmi and Cacace have listed a series of signs that should make parents worry:

- sudden depression of mood;
- disinterest in school;
- decreased ability to concentrate;
- restlessness, aggression, sudden changes in mood;
- hostile rebellion;
- tendency to loneliness;
- sudden drop in school performance;
- changing interests and regular friends;
- interest in mythology, magic, rituals and symbolism;
- interest in the contents of violent, bloody occult;
- attraction for what is mysterious;
- excessive refusal of the religious values of one's parents.

Obviously, in order to notice these warning signs and intervene accordingly, it is essential that parents speak and dialogue with their sons and daughters, that they spend a lot of time together and share the experience of growth. Give them an emotional and psychic space in which they can feel understood. Talk with them, give them advice, discuss, listen, show attention to their problems and interests, so that they always feel welcomed and free to be able to share their thoughts and anxieties about what can happen. Since no teenager takes refuge in extreme conduct without having first manifested his suffering in some way, if this type of relationship is established, it will be easier for parents to identify the problems of their children and change their wrong paths. Let's remember this.

Chapter Nine
"Sectarian culture and crime"

"Life can get ugly when you turn 80,
especially if there is a police car behind you."

SAM EWING

Without us realizing it, without paying particular attention to it, precisely because we are used to it, we are surrounded by references to esotericism, the occult, magic (white or black), witchcraft, paganism and Satanism. Books, magazines, television, music, the web and cinema talk about it.

Books

The number of books dedicated to new religious movements is constantly growing, so much so that there are more and more libraries dedicated only to this kind of texts. The occult is fascinating, and often teenagers start to be interested in reading small novels that base their plot on the events of small religious sects, on witchcraft or on the use of magic. They are cheap novels that are easily available, even in supermarkets. Sometimes they are so engaging that they are used as an example by small groups of young people to define their religious purposes, names, goals and powers of the members. The groups of young Satanists are inspired by texts of various kinds, sometimes even by school books, especially by the great classics of literature (Carducci, Baudelaire, Milton) in which the figure of Satan appears, from comics, from videogames and from role-playing games.

The most popular book among all those who decide to become Satanists is Anton Sznador LaVey's *The Satanic Bible*, cheap and easily available. Other widely used books are *The Satanic Rituals*, also by LaVey, the *Malleus Maleficarum* by H. Kramer and J. Sprenger, the most famous texts by Aleister Crowley, such as *Magick* and *The Book of the Law*, and the most famous black magic text, *The Black Arts* by Richard Cavendish. Also for those who decide to be a Satanist, the most important book of all is perhaps their own *Book of Darkness* (Barresi 2006), which is nothing more than their own personal diary, in which to collect the rituals performed, the magic formulas, the rules of one's sect. *The Book of Darkness* is personalized by every Satanist, sometimes it is written in reverse to make it encrypted, jealously guarded, decorated and covered with magical powers.

Items

There are also criminogenic items: without them it is not possible to participate in satanic rites. According to what is described in LaVey's Satanic Bible, to participate in satanic rites it is essential to wear a tunic with a hood (black or blood red or purple), handmade by each owner, to be worn alone, without any other garment . Depending on how organized the groups of Satanists are, they will need isolated places in which to gather, an altar (which often consists of a mattress), candles, consecrated hosts to be desacralized and anything else necessary for their rites. Sado-masochist satanic groups, for example, will need - which take the form of large organized orgies - latex suits, whips, collars, masks, sex toys, chains and studs.

Music

Music is one of the most powerful means of expression and aggregation for young people. Through music it is possible to communicate and share. Black and death metal music, if listened by already alienated, frustrated and marginalized young people, pushes them towards anti-social conduct. It conveys content that is contrary to socially shared and adaptive values: it communicates violence, selfishness, rebellion, aggression, abuse of power and apathy. In addition, it brings you closer to the world of acid Satanism, which we know is very dangerous.

Unlike the satanic rock of the 80s and 90s, today the music that is used by satanic groups is mostly electronic music. Electronic music has sounds capable of stimulating certain areas of the cerebral cortex that release endorphins. It is a psychic drug. It is able to alter the listener's state of consciousness, even more if under the influence of drugs. Some types of electronic music, such as techno, have a syncopated rhythm that imitates the heartbeat and very low tones and vibrations, which are listened to at a very high volume, so that they reverberate in the body and make the internal organs vibrate, especially those in the pelvic area.

They are a natural aphrodisiac. In fact, these genres of music are listened to during the orgiastic phases of satanic rites, they help to let go and get completely lost. Many electronic artists, often for market needs, accompany their music with texts idolizing Satan and other evil demons.

Cinema and television

In the past, cinema and television in the western world were exclusive means of communication, reserved only for that part of the population that could afford them, while today they have a universal diffusion. It is difficult not to find a TV in a house, and if you do not have it, it is because of a choice, not because of economic impossibility. Then there is the internet, thanks to which you can stream all the films you want. Needless to say how many films have been made with reference to demons or witches, how many horror movies have been made to date, where it is possible to witness violent and bloody scenes, where it is the same spectator who seeks mental and emotional terror, suspense and brutal images. In this kind of film evil is often not manifest, it remains suspended and furtive. It creeps into the mind of the viewer, who ends up wanting it, imagining it and wanting to see it manifest in the film. Evil is, in the end, mocking and victorious. Television is even more dangerous than cinema, since it offers us hidden contents without us having chosen them. The programming is full of allusions and occult practices, spells, reincarnations, magic and supernatural forces. The magical world that is presented is often an unproblematic world, in which magic allows the protagonists to solve all daily problems. Then, the programs that are broadcast today, have a different ethical content from the fairy tales that were read to us as children. Good and evil are no longer so clearly distinguishable, it is no longer good that fights against evil and overcomes it. The outlines today are blurred. The programs presented to children have a relativistic conception of good and evil: there is a neutral force that can be used for both good and evil purposes. Think of the TV series «Charmed», which has important contents from a criminogenic point of view. The three witches are ordinary people, who live the same everyday world as all of us, but with magical powers. It is white magic, because the three witches fight against evil. We continually witness spells that can change the fate of the protagonists, and magic eventually takes on a positive value. However, for the three girls to continue using magic, they must necessarily move away from their social relationships. They cannot have friends for fear that they will discover their secret; in the same way, they never see their family, they work for short periods and they don't go to school. Social isolation. Maybe we don't realize it immediately, but the impact and the suggestion that this TV series and other TV programs can have on younger people is not to be underestimated. The influence of the occult in today's television and cinema exists, and it is certainly very subtle and penetrating. Young people, without knowing it, undergo important criminogenic influences. Furthermore, being continuously exposed to strong, raw and violent images, albeit simulated and unreal, generates an emotional anesthesia in the adolescent that makes him unable to react in case of violent or criminal episodes in real life. He tolerates them, sometimes he justifies them.

Special content: "Heaven's Gate"

There is no scientific evidence for the presence of alien entities in the Universe, much less their numbered messages to the Earth Protocol Office. Despite this, man has always wondered what is above his head, in that gray-blue sky by day and dotted with satellites at night. There are many hypotheses that alien civilizations dart on ships and come into contact with mankind: some testimonies report a "divine" attitude on the part of these extraterrestrial entities, which bring messages of peace and prosperity to us, but which also bring apocalyptic and eschatological sentences on the fate of the Earth (death penalty or life imprisonment?). What we certainly know, however, is that the United States is the land with the highest percentage of sightings and contacts of the third type: we do not often find aliens on the Via Aurelia or walking barefoot on the way to Santiago. Aliens in the US have often been incorporated into the humus of the society of the time and have become the fundamental basis of some millennial religions that have spread like wildfire, even crossing the

US border. The causes that gave rise to the birth of these religions are many. One of the many relates to the fact that man organizes himself by colonies and, net of evident social problems, has a critical need for aggregation. Heaven's Gate, the ufological religion based in Rancho Santa Fe, California, is certainly born from these needs. A deadly cocktail of mystical beliefs, psychiatric/psychological problems, social disorders, jams of important mechanisms of the bio-psychosocial machine of founders and their followers. Heaven's Gate was born from the particular encounter between Bonnie Lu Trousdale Nettles and Marshall "Herff" Applewhite. She is a graduate nurse who works in a hospital in Houston, Texas, married to children with a particular passion for esoteric rites; he is the son of Presbyterian pastor Marshall Herff Applewhite Senior, of whom he will try to follow in the footsteps.

A graduate in music studies from the University of Colorado, Herff combines his passion for music with that of spirituality. After a noteworthy musical career for those times, he became a music teacher at the University of Alabama. Married and father of two children, Herff is consumed by his homosexuality, which he kept hidden from his family and colleagues, but which eventually became known. He will be left by his wife and will also lose his job as a professor. Marshall "Herff" Applewhite is depressed and is also abandoned by the Presbyterian community, which will never forgive him for his homosexual relationships, let alone his shaky religiosity, far from his father. Herff descends the dark, winding steps of his soul, throwing himself, hungry and unsatisfied, on music, without finding peace. Then he falls prey to the usual demons and, due to sentimental problems with a girl with whom he was about to get married, he is forced to flee Houston, wandering in various cities, from New York to Mexico City. Between 1971 and 1972 he was hospitalized several times for mental problems also due to his disastrous economic condition and on one of these occasions, in March 1972, he met Bonnie with whom he immediately established, as we said above, a friendship linked by common passions on ufological and esoteric - religious questions.

Thus the two embark on the path to the foundation of Heaven's Gate. Applewhite and Nettles leave Houston, travel from city to city and then the electrocution: they feel the need to take a trip to the desert to try to define their spirituality. Here, worthy of the History and the Prophets that Humanity has seen before them, the two say they have come into contact with extraterrestrial entities that would have commanded (imperative and obligation) them to spread a message regarding the apocalyptic fate of the universe , that is, its total collapse. Only the chosen few would have been saved by these aliens, who would have brought them to safety in a spaceship. Once out of the desert, the two begin their mission and so the doctrine of the sect begins to take shape. Access to this New Life is regulated by stringent rules, such as flexibility, denial of primary needs (food, emotional relationships, contacts with the outside etc.). A free and promiscuous sexuality among the components and, above all, complete devotion to be demonstrated through the mutual and daily control of the actions between the companions. Each adept must seek purity in his soul, redeem himself and leave his power in the hands of future saviors. This would have given them a place on the ship.

The flight, which according to Applewhite's calculations was getting closer, made it necessary to gather as many faithful as possible. The Heaven's Gate community expanded between the 1980s and 1990s, and spread its creed throughout the United States, embarking on a sort of millennial crusade for the whole country. To finance travel, conferences and locations in Wyoming, Nettles and Applewhite founded a web design company, Higher Resource, which specialized in creating Internet pages; this activity attracts many investors and therefore contributes to the spread of the verb. In 1985 Nettles died of breast cancer: Applewhite thus became the only leader in command (Benjamin E. Zeller, Heaven's Gate: America's UFO Religion, New York University Press, New York, 2014). After years of expansion and inclusion with new members from all over the country, Applewhite decides to promote a more exclusive and secret attitude for the sect. The leader thus gathers all his followers in the new official residence located in Rancho Santa Fe, near San Diego, California, where the prohibitions begin to increase and tighten.

From androgynous clothing to brushed hair, the faithful are disciplined by means of self-control and passivity, inculcated in their daily behavior by strict mutual controls between the members themselves. Each member had to meet another comrade every 12 minutes to avoid actions that could question the general rules, thus jeopardizing collective well-being. And then comes 1995: almost 20 years of waiting have passed and the signal of the aliens, so longed for, is revealed to all believers, with the passage of the comet Hale -Bopp. On that occasion, NASA took a photo from the Hubble Space Telescope which revealed the presence of "a connection of matter" in the comet's wake; but only in 1996 there was talk of a real UFO (unidentified flying object). In January 1997 Heaven's Gate screams out a dispatch via the internet claiming that whatever it is, it will catastrophically affect this planet. "It is the sign that the planet is about to be reset. It is also our exit offer for the awakened ones who follow it: to leave this world to survive", (Massimo Introvigne, Heaven's Gate - heaven cannot wait, Editrice ElleDiCi, Turin, 1997). The declaration ends with the revelation of the spacecraft (what seemed to be the mysterious agglomeration of matter) that came to take the members of the group, and that its passage would have been short; once the passage to Heaven's Gate was lost, it would close definitively. Time is running out and Applewhite acts by implementing the plan agreed years ago with its faithful partner Nettles, namely to take that "transition" at all costs and by any means possible. On March 19, the leader and his companions record videos as a final farewell which they will send by mail to their families. Dressed in black, with sports shoes, brush hair and ready backpacks, the members of Heaven's Gate begin the ascension process (Gary A. Beck, Heaven's Gate - A Memorial, AuthorHouse, Bloomington, 2009).

They end the life of their earthly bodies by ingesting Phenobarbitals mixed with solid food; they drink huge quantities of vodka and lie down in their beds waiting to die and go to the other side. Some of the members seal their heads, at the base of the neck, with plastic bags securing them with adhesive tape, thus being able to end up suffocated in case they have awakened from the deadly cocktail. About a week after the suicide the local authorities break the doors of the villa in Rancho Santa Fe - warned by the owner of the villa, unable to contact the tenants - and bring to light a gruesome show: 39 dead people (21 women and 18 men), including Applewhite. The bodies are already in a decomposition phase and the forensic doctors who perform the autopsies report disturbing details of the fatal day: the faithful committed suicide in stages, slowly waiting for their turn and covering the deceased, from time to time, with purple shrouds. In the pockets of each of them are found 5 dollars in coins, perhaps convinced of their need even in the new world. Evidently the concept of death as the total end of existence has not embraced this pseudo-ufological religion, convinced instead that emptying the "container", or abandoning one's body, was a necessary step to access the truths proposed and assimilated over the years. The suicide had international resonance and created a heated debate (perhaps still unresolved).

Chapter Ten

"How to become a Satanist: mental manipulation"

"There is only one sin, only one. And that is theft.
Every other sin is a variation of theft."
KHALED HOSSEINI

Joining a satanic sect means undergoing a process of mental manipulation. All members of the sect, from newly-adopted to leaders, undergo this process. Mental manipulation is possible in a situation where the relationship is asymmetrical: there must be one person with greater power than the others. Thanks to his position of power, the leader is able to exploit the victim's identity for his own purposes, threatening the victim's integrity and autonomy, and making the victim almost totally dependent on himself and his will. The identity of each individual is a sum of beliefs, experiences, emotions and beliefs that derive from one's life path. Through the path of mental manipulation it is possible to "overwrite" a new group identity, which responds to the needs of the cult. Adepts undergo a precise mental manipulation technique, which can be divided into five phases:

- recruitment;
- initiation to the doctrine;
- rooting in the group;
- removal from society and isolation;
- strengthening the doctrine.

Recruitment

The members of the group in charge of proselytizing never turn to a stranger in a disinterested way: their goal is always to attract someone to their own sect. From the first contact, the victim begins to suffer an initial emotional disorientation: the victim's beliefs are put into crisis, she is shown how her own happiness is fictitious, as this happiness is subjugated by an infinite series of moral norms and cultural conditioning typical of a ruined society. Being in difficulty and unable to fight back, the victim is at fault and is often convinced to be present at a first sectarian meeting. Once inside the sect, the newcomer finds himself immersed in an artificial world made of happiness, warm and welcoming atmospheres, a harmonious and friendly group, which almost does not seem to be part of this world. The need to feel part of something and to feel safe is immediately satisfied. The sectarian group is the answer to all problems. Within the sect, the new adept is approached by the elders of the group, who tell him how much their life has changed for the better, how much they lived in the illusion of being happy and how much they really are now, thanks to this path of liberation and conversion that led them to discover the truth and give meaning to their lives.

A recruiting technique widely used within satanic sects, given the extreme importance that sex has within these sects, is flirty fishing: girls have the task of seducing boys and girls through love flirts, and they have also the task of drawing up a weekly report in which they communicate how many new boys they have managed to recruit.

Initiation to doctrine

Once part of the group, the adept is indoctrinated. He must read books, watch videos, attend meetings, seminars, listen to the leader or senior members. In the first phase of indoctrination, which is administered in small doses, the neophyte undergoes the so-called "love bomb": he is filled with affection, compliments and affectionate gratifications. Even his agenda is filled with commitments. All this affection and all this time spent together with the other members of the sect prevents the individual from having time to critically reflect on the doctrine that they are inculcating in him. He experiences a confusing state that leads him to self-suggestion: the desire to remain part of the group and to find this promised truth leads him not to build a critical knowledge. He doesn't care if his friends or family don't believe it, if there are pessimists and skeptics who mock him. He wants to go all the way because he has found a world where everyone loves him and protects him, and where he knows he will always be happy. In the second phase of indoctrination, after the adept's will has been completely subdued, the chief and senior members implement a strategy based on affective frustration.

The objectives that the follower must achieve are moved further and further, so as to generate in him a series of disappointments, to which the group turns its back. The reaction that is generated in the adept is that of dependence: he will lose confidence in himself and will be led to react by participating even more frequently and intensely in the group's activities and ideology. It is clear, for those who know it, that within this type of group the same dynamics of Stockholm Syndrome are created, in which an individual, who is in a condition of dependence on another (for example hostage and kidnapper), transforms the natural feeling of resentment and contempt into a feeling of affection and admiration, precisely because of this addiction. Frustration and disappointment can only be overcome by adopting a new cult identity, which must inevitably replace the previous one. The cultural, critical and experiential background of the adept is destroyed and restructured in a way more suited to the needs of the sectarian group.

Rooting in the group

We are in the most delicate phase. At this point the adept is completely inserted in the sect, the good times when he was pampered and guided step by step in the indoctrination are over. Now he is completely immersed in the hard and frenetic daily life of the sect, between missionary activities, work in the center, getting money and the continuous rites and rituals. He is inserted into an uninterrupted work program, so that he does not have time for individual needs. He must change all his life habits and devote all his energies to respond to the group's requests. Sometimes the group prescribes members to deprive themselves of sleep, to fast or to follow strict diets. In this way the person experiences a psycho-physical condition of weakness, which does not allow him to question himself critically about what is happening to him or about the cult he is so fervently trusting. The psychological pressure exerted by the leader and the group increases more and more, and when the individual member fails to meet the needs of the group he is humiliated and, at times, punished. To uncertainty, inadequacy and the feeling of not feeling up to it, the adept responds by continuing to adapt and submit, increasing his commitment and discipline. His will is broken and subjugated to sectarian needs. It's not just a losing game, however.

As compensation for all frustrations, members are guaranteed security: they no longer have daily worries, the sect will take care of all their worries, even those for the future and for what they have left outside the sect. Another very effective strategy for making newbies rooted in the group is to engage in missionary activities and recruit new followers. Having to convince strangers of the positive effects and truth of their doctrine, they must first of all believe it themselves. Without realizing it, in this way the members manipulate and condition their own conscience. Here is a list of a series of behaviors put in place by the leaders of satanic sects to manipulate the minds of adepts:

a) Isolation. Getting people away from social support increases their psychological dependence on the leader;

b) Manipulation of perception. It can be implemented through the lack or excess of light, or by particular types of diet. It induces attention to current problems and increases introspective activity. It can also be used as a punishment for disobedience;

c) Induction of physical weakness. By means of sleep deprivation, poor diet, physical hyperactivity, it aims to weaken the mental and physical capacity to resist;

d) Threats. They generate anxiety and despair, much more than the action itself;

e) Occasional indulgences. They are sporadic favors and rewards, which prevent the individual from adapting to deprivation;

f) Degradation. These are humiliating conditions in which the individual is forced to stay (for example the deprivation of intimate hygiene), which lead to a decrease in self-esteem and an increase in awe;

g) Trivial requests. They aim to develop obedience;

h) Hyperventilation. A phenomenon that is called "respiratory alkalosis" (which can also cause fainting), which consist in screaming or chanting phrases or slogans aloud with deep expirations, causing large volumes of air to pass in and out of the lungs. After shouting for a long time, people have very slow, poor breathing to compensate for previous respiratory excesses and restore a chemical balance of the blood. The person feels weak, exhausted, aware of having lived a dramatic and upsetting experience.

There is no doubt that mental manipulation is the ideal tool for obtaining the psychological control of an individual, even pushing him to commit crimes that, on a conscious level, he probably would never have committed.

Removal from society and isolation

When the follower has managed to resist and has taken root in the group, it is possible to continue the manipulation by moving him away from society and its past. Isolation pursues the aim of protecting members from all the unpleasant influences of the outside world, so as to continue to make them available for the purposes of the sect. In this phase the members of the group denigrate all the emotional relationships that the individual lived outside, and all the values transmitted to him by society. He is prevented from talking about the sect with relatives and friends. They wouldn't understand, or maybe they would hinder him. Too risky. All the life experiences that the subject lived before joining the cult are devalued, especially on an emotional level, since they were experiences lived within an aimless, meaningless existence. Only the experiences conducted within the sect make sense, have emotional value and deserve attention and emotional participation.

Strengthening the doctrine

In the fifth and final phase the mechanisms of dependence are refined, to complete the control of conscience and to strengthen the identity of the sect. This is possible by continuing the rituals and indoctrination, even of elderly members, at an almost exhausting rate. In doing so, the indoctrinators try to prevent psycho-physical exhaustion from resurfacing the individual identity of individual members and doubts about the life that they are living. Insulation must also be kept under control. In some sects there is even complete control of information. Members are completely prohibited from consulting the mass media, all their exchanges with the external environment are controlled, phone calls and messages to their family members, (ex) friends or other external people are strictly forbidden. Leaving the sect is difficult because through involvement in increasingly transgressive rituals, which make the adept complicit in immoral or anti-law practices, psychological control is constantly reinforced, to guarantee total loyalty to the sect. However, it is a fact that some members manage to leave the sect. For them, the path back to reality is very painful, and sometimes important psychological disorders arise. The original personal identity is not eliminated, as mentioned at the beginning of the paragraph, but is "overwritten"; slowly, the memories, emotions and perceptions of life resurface. However, this is a difficult path, so it is advisable to be accompanied by an expert. In the fifth edition of the DSM, "Dissociative disorder with other specification" was introduced, where the symptoms of dissociative disorder remain (manifestations of anxiety, phobias, panic attacks, eating disorders, sexual dysfunctions, feeling of unreality, estrangement from one's own self, different perception of the environment, of people, family and non-family members, as if they were unknown, doubts and identity loss), in relation to which the Manual also introduced "Identity disturbance due to prolonged and intense coercive persuasion". This disorder is described as: "individuals who have been subjected to intense coercive persuasions (for example: brainwashing, re-education, indoctrination during periods of imprisonment, torture, long political detentions, involvement in sects/cults or terrorist organizations) can manifest prolonged changes in one's identity". Philippe Parquet has developed, in this regard, a specific grid of criteria, within which at least 5 of the 9 must be found, in order to affirm that there is an ongoing mental conditioning:

1. Break with the methods of previous behavior and judgment, with values, individual, family and collective social relationships;

2. Break with the previous life and acceptance by the individual that his personality, his affective, cognitive, rational, moral and social life are shaped by suggestions, injunctions, orders, ideas, concepts, values and doctrines imposed by a third party or institution;

3. Adhesion and unconditional loyalty; affective, behavioral, intellectual, moral and social loyalty to a person, group or institution;

4. Complete, progressive and total availability of one's life to a person, group or institution;

5. Heightened sensitivity to the ideas, concepts, prescriptions, injunctions and orders of a doctrine, and possibly the use of these in proselytizing practices;

6. Expropriation of a person's abilities, with affective anesthesia, alteration of judgment, loss of references, values and critical spirit;

7. Alteration of freedom of choice;

8. Impermeability to opinions, attitudes, values of the external environment, with the impossibility of promoting change;

9. Inducement to carry out acts which are seriously prejudicial to the person, acts which previously were not part of the subject's life. These acts are no longer perceived as harmful or in contrast with the values and customs generally accepted by society. Sometimes participation in a sect results in psychiatric disorder, other times psychological support is needed.

We have seen what are the social and psychological factors that push a person to take an interest in sects and new religious groups. Not all groups of Satanists can be called sects, because sects have very specific characteristics. They are characterized primarily by this process of mental manipulation, and then by the other characteristics of its rigid and pyramidal structure, by the presence of a leader and by closure towards the outside world. Some groups of Satanists remain simple groups of people who share the same unease and desires, and sometimes small groups are far more dangerous than the big organized sects.

To be continued.

Readings strictly recommended in the volume and bibliography.

- American Psychiatric Association, DSM-5.

- Up. Blanchot M. (2003) Lautreamont e Sade, SE.

- Crowley A., The book of the law, Red Wheel/Weiser, 2004.

- Der Alptraum in seiner Beziehung zu gewissen Formen des mittelalterlichen Aberglaubens, in Schriften zur Angewandten Seelenkunde, XIV (7), Newton Compton, 1978.

- Goldberg A. (1995) The problem of perversion, Yale University Press, New Haven.

- Der Doppelgünger, in Imago, III, 1914, SugarCo, 1967.

- LaVey A., The Satanic Bible, Avon Books, 1969.

- "Current Methods in Forensic Gunshot Residue Analysis", A.J. Schwoeble, D.L. Exline.-

- "Criminal profiling", Scotia J. Hicks, Bruce D. Sales.

- "Profilers: leading investigators take you inside the criminal mind", Campbell J. & De Nevi D.

- "Cold Case Research Resources for Unidentified, Missing, and Cold Homicide Cases", Silvia Pettem.

- "Profiling Violent Crimes: An Investigative Tool", Ronald M. Holmes e Stephen T. Holmes.

- "Mindhunter", John Douglas, Mark Olshaker.

- "Fingerprint Identification", William Leo.

- "CriminologiaOggi da Beccaria ai Social" Esposito Francesco

666. the Ghost Book

Satanic Crimes + Black Criminology for beginners

CHAPTER ONE

SATANISM, THE GENESIS OF EVIL

Satanism, definitions and history

> *"Please allow me to introduce myself*
>
> *I'm a man of wealth and taste*
>
> *I've been around for a long, long year*
>
> *Stole many a man's soul to waste"*
>
> *(Rolling Stones - Sympathy For The Devil)*

According to the common imagination, Satanists are people dressed in black, with long hair, who listen to heavy metal. Satanists gather in the woods, in cemeteries and in deconsecrated churches to perform their rituals, such as slaughtering animals, drinking their blood, saying mass on the contrary, insulting God, up to human sacrifice. They can be recognized by the number 666 (in the New Testament, the Book of Revelation asserts 666 to be "man's number" or "the number of a man" associated with the Beast, and since seven is a number of completeness and is associated with the divine, six is incomplete and the three sixes are inherently incomplete), by the inverted pentacle, by the Baphomet and by the reversed cross (the so-called Cross of Saint Peter, initially a Christian symbol which later became an emblem of Satanism). But beyond the common imagination there is a different reality. First of all, the modern Satanist can belong to various types of sects, all very different from each other. If we wanted to give a simple and generic description, however, we could define the modern Satanist as an ego-centered individual. All beliefs and rituals are used to please and celebrate the needs of one's ego, needs related to sex, power and wealth. In this sense, Satanism rejects Christianity, which on the contrary is considered the religion of limitations and abstinence, which dictates the rules of good and evil. The Satanist instead rejects an absolute distinction between Good and Evil; they are relative concepts, therefore every human being is free to distinguish them as he prefers. It is about individualism in its most extreme form, in which the good corresponds to what is useful to one's interests; everything else is bad, and for the Satanist it is unthinkable that someone from outside decides on it. It is in this perspective that rituals, spells and sacrifices are inserted, aimed at satisfying one's needs. The sacrifices foreseen in the satanic rites are four (Cantelmi, Cacace 2007, p. 50): the sacrifice of oneself, inflicting pain on oneself, offering parts of dead animals or human beings, and offering parts of living animals or human beings. Immolating oneself to Satan is possible through masturbation, oral sex and sexual practices, both straight and homosexual. Sacrificing oneself by inflicting pain means cutting one's arms, thighs and buttocks with razors or sharp knives. To sacrifice parts of dead animals, it is sufficient to recover corpses on the side of roads or wild places; human bones instead are recovered in cemeteries. Finally, sacrificing a live animal is necessary when the vital energy of the animal itself is fundamental for the effectiveness of the ritual. The killing of live human beings for sacrificial purposes is rather rare, but not to be underestimated. Satanism is a phenomenon on which several scholars have interrogated themselves. According to M. Introvigne's definition (2010, p. 13), Satanism - from a historical and sociological point of view - can be defined as "adoration or veneration, by groups organized in the form of movement, through repeated cultural or liturgical practices of the character called Satan or Devil in the Bible, whether this is intended as a person or as a mere symbol". This definition is deliberately generic, since modern Satanism is a multifaceted and complex phenomenon, which includes a large number of beliefs, all attributable to the figure of Satan. Even theology, inevitably, had to deal with Satanism. Theology defines Satanists as "all those groups that manifest aversion or hatred towards God and at the same time propose to man to become like God using magical and occult practices" (ibid). This reading of Satanism is legitimate and necessary in the context of theology, but for the purposes of our criminological study we believe it is correct to adopt the historical-sociological definition.

1.1. Occultism, Esotericism, Satanism, Witchcraft, Sabbath

"There is not an individual who is the devil. You could say the opposite of good is the devil, and that is in every one of us. It is just the selfish, greedy personality expression of individuals."

Benjamin Crème - The Ageless Wisdom, An Introduction to Humanity's Spiritual Legacy, (1996), p. 33)

The word "Satanism" recalls many other terms, such as esotericism, occultism and witchcraft. But, as you can imagine, each term refers to different concepts. Today when we speak of esotericism we generally refer to all the mystical doctrines having, as a general characteristic, secrecy and confidentiality (Perrotta 2016, p. 20). If you look for the word "esoteric" on the Treccani Encyclopedia, you read: "the doctrines and secret teachings, which must not be divulged because they are intended for the few". In reality, esotericism was originally nothing more than the set of studies on nature from the original perspective of the cult of origins (ibid, p. 22). It is the study of nature at 360°, a global science, which embraces all the human sciences, from medicine to psychology, up to mathematics and technology. It is represented by the ancient doctor, pharmacist, chemist and herbalist - popularly called "sorcerer" - who cured, thanks to nature, all known pathologies. It includes all studies on the internal nature of man which lead, through introspection, to the rediscovery of ourselves, to the knowledge of our "internal nature", of God and of Truth. It was during the Enlightenment that esotericism and occultism were confused and included in a single whole, within which esotericism was associated with hidden knowledge (from the Latin «*occultus*», hidden). According to the conception of that time, in fact, esoteric sciences, such as alchemy, had to hide, become hidden through allegories, in order not to suffer the reactions (even violent) of the Church which, to ensure power, was declared the only holder of the Truth and the word of God. During this period therefore the term esotericism began to be used incorrectly and was associated with disciplines, beliefs and superstitions of an irrational nature. Before then, all esoteric disciplines had kept well away from anything that could not be guided by logic and reason. From then on, however, ancient disciplines such as astrology and alchemy[1], voodoo[2] and popular beliefs, cabal[3], magic rites and numerology[4] were dusted off, which contaminated the esotericism of new surreal concepts, introducing modern terms of "paranormal" and "supernatural". All this confusion led, in the 16th and 17th centuries AD, to the famous times of the inquisition and the witch hunt. Witchcraft was associated with the worship of the devil, and therefore condemned. In this period magical art is assimilated to occult witchcraft practices and evil, the historical enemy of good, is identified in the Devil. Here then, we have Satanism. In the Christian sphere, in the fifteenth and sixteenth centuries, the term "Satanism" indicates the popular beliefs linked to the rites of devotion, adoration and evocation of Lucifer and other demons (all considered acts of witchcraft). Satanism and witchcraft have consequently become synonymous. Of course this does not mean that witchcraft and Satanism are the same thing. The word witchcraft "indicates a set of magical practices aimed at assuring those who perform them an influence on people or things that goes beyond the ordinary principle of causality" (Introvinge 2010, p. 22). In traditional witchcraft, magic is used to do harm, do good or transform the attitude of outsiders towards the applicant. Magic is used outwards. In modern witchcraft, the so called Wicca, magic is used instead to obtain changes, especially at the psychological level, of the operator. Magic is used inward. And where is the Devil? Already from the classical Greek-Latin world we have evidence of magical practices that referred to pagan spirits and deities. Over the centuries, witchcraft remained, but the spirits to turn to for the rites of white and black magic changed[5]. With the advent of Christianity, pagan deities were gradually transformed into infernal creatures and therefore badly seen by the Church. The direct references to the devil, however, are found only in the Sabbath, a ritual in which witches and sorcerers gather to celebrate the Devil in his presence. In the Sabbath, orgies are practiced, banquets of human flesh are held, the Christian religion is denied and one is baptized in the diabolical faith. It is organized in remote and uncrowded places, such as cemeteries, isolated mountain peaks or remote clearings[6]. Several times witchcraft has been accused of making pacts with the Devil to give greater efficacy to their rituals, accusations that still remain. Contemporary Wicca continues to defend itself against these accusations by replying that its devotion is not addressed at all to the Devil, but to other pre-Christian divinities. In traditional witchcraft, which is less widespread today but still not extinct, it is instead possible to ask the sorcerer, to make the rite more effective, to invoke the Devil.

1.2. Historical cycles of Satanism

"We are each our own devil, and we make this world our hell."
(Oscar Wilde)

The first historical references regarding Satanism date back to the 16th and 17th centuries. M. Introvigne, sociologist and historian of religions, studied its history and noted that, like many other historical phenomena, the cult of Satan has had a cyclical trend over the centuries, divided into three phases (2010, p. 14):

a) in the first phase, the Satanist movements arise in opposition to the majority cultural styles, highlighting their contradictions and paradoxes. The movement, often thanks to the charismatic personality of its leader, spreads in a short time;

b) in the second phase, the majority, secular and religious cultures take note of the existence of these movements and do not accept seeing all their own contradictions mirrored. They begin by ostracizing them, criminalizing and boycotting them in various ways. What seems to be most effective, as it manages to affect public opinion the most, is the testimony of repentant Satanists, who tell frightening, gruesome and unthinkable episodes, which inevitably intrigue the bored people;

c) in the third phase, the struggle of the anti-Satanists no longer holds because, in order to scandalize, the confessions of repentant Satanists become so extreme as to be surreal. The activity of many journalists ends up exposing the stories of these characters, who are then held up as imposters or mythomaniacs.

Finally the anti-Satanist war ends because it becomes a one-way confrontation. The Satanists, unable to play on equal terms, end up hiding and reducing their visibility. It is the perfect strategy so that public opinion is no longer interested in anti-Satanist campaigns and minorities in dissent with the dominant culture organize themselves into new satanic movements. Thus the cycle begins again.

1.3. The first black mass in history

"Son, the greatest trick the Devil pulled was convincing the world there was only one of him."(David Wong, John Dies at the End)

We are at the court of Louis XIV in Paris in the 17th century. History teaches us that in those days moral corruption was anything but pointed out and blamed. The sovereign himself had a long line of lovers, and curiosity for esotericism and the occult sciences had already been widespread for some time. It is in this context that we find Catherine Deshayes, known as La Voisin, court dealer who leaded a profitable trade in cosmetics and medicines among the noblewomen closest to the king. In addition to the legitimate sale of these products, La Voisin also offered poisons, clandestine abortions, astrological forecasts and consecrated hosts (in those days it was believed that the use of consecrated hosts gave particular powers during demonic rites). In 1666 the first cycle of black Masses of history begins at the La Voisin house, in a chapel with black drapes hanging on the black walls and black candles made of human fat.[7] Instead of the altar, there was a mattress, on which rested a naked woman, who received kisses between the legs by the priest, who then slipped the consecrated host into her and then had sex with her. The Black Mass was born as an overthrow of the Catholic Mass. Just as in the Catholic rite there is the moment of the offertory in which bread (hosts) and wine are offered to the celebrant, who blesses God for the gifts received and then offers them to all the disciples, so in the black Mass a sacrifice is made at the time of the offertory. From the testimonies, it seems that doves and children were immolated. For the sacrifice of children the fetuses of the abortions (which were practiced secretly) were initially used; then children killed on purpose, children of common people, kidnapped by the members of the group. From other testimonies it seems that the participants of the Mass had to drink an elixir containing semen and menstrual blood. The use of consecrated hosts, the woman as an altar and the consumption of the elixir are characteristic of all the black Masses held below and the black Masses still practiced today. This is the reason why we can consider the La Voisin case the first historical event attributable to Satanism, as the liturgies were organized continuously by a group of people (which today we would call "sect") and because a real Black Mass ritual was created , amalgamating the traditions left behind by witchcraft and other esoteric cults. However, if formally this episode is associated with Satanism, it is more difficult to consider it in substance. Voisin and her followers were not really devoted to Satan in a religious sense, much less they wanted the extinction of Christianity. For them the worship of Satan was utilitarian, linked only and exclusively to material ends; Voisin, in fact, became very rich. The Black Mass, the sale of poisons, consecrated hosts and the practice of hidden abortions became a very profitable business, but devoid of any free devotion to Satan as a divinity.

1.4. Classical Satanism, 19th and 20th centuries

"People who cease to believe in God or goodness altogether still believe in the devil ... Evil is always possible. And goodness is eternally difficult." (Anne Rice, Interview with the Vampire)

After an initial period of interest and growth about the satanic cult, starting in the 1860s theologians, writers, intellectuals and politicians began a real anti-Satanist campaign. The goal was to seek Satanism everywhere, in literary publications, in traditions, in newspaper articles, in other religions. Relations with the Devil were also found in Freemasonry, Kabbalah and Mormonism. The polemicists were so busy trying to find Satanism everywhere that they forgot to investigate the black Masses and the most obvious forms of the cult of Satan. In an attempt to seek and condemn the unwitting Satanists, they forgot to look for the conscious ones, the pure and militant ones. Between 1870 and 1890 it was not the professional anti-Satanists who noticed the existence of small but important forms of Satanism inspired by La Voisin, but the curious on the occult, such as the writer Joris-Karl Huysmans and the journalist Jules Bois. Huysmans was one of the first French decadent writers; together with his friend Jules Bois, journalist passionate about Eastern religions and esotericism, he collected a lot of material for his novel Là-Bas ("The abyss"), which became a real best seller, known to this day. Central to the novel is the figure of Gilles de Rais, known for his involvement in alchemical and occult practices in which he tortured, raped and killed at least 140 children and adolescents.

"The devil can do nothing against the will, very little on intelligence and all on fantasy." (Joris Karl Huysmans)

The sincere worshiper of Satan is, according to Huysmans, the one who believes in the Devil of the Bible and decides to take his side.

With his research, the author made known all the contradictions that Satanists found both in the culture of the secular and anticlerical world and in the culture of the Catholic religion. The refusal to accept these contradictions as true by the majority culture and the fear for all these groups of people, who remained hidden, generated a strong social alarm, which gave rise to another phase of anti-Satanism. At the beginning of the twentieth century we find Aleister Crowley, a name known to anyone who has studied Satanism. In reality, Crowley was not at all a Satanist, on the contrary, he was an atheist, yet his writings greatly influenced the twentieth century Satanism. Indeed "it can be said that without Crowley the Satanism of the twentieth and twenty-first centuries would not exist" (Introvigne 2010, p. 210). His reputation as a Satanist is mainly due to theologians, given that anyone who opposes Christianity and enhances sexuality falls within their definition of Satanist. According to the historical and sociological definition of Satanism made by Devigne, in order for a person or group to be defined as Satanist, it is necessary that he worship Satan through cults and rituals. It is not enough to cite it or exhibit some of its symbols, otherwise we should consider all those writers who have used his name over the centuries to refer to the concept of rebellion, anticlericalism, transgression, rationalism and so on as Satanists. In this sense Crowley is not a Satanist, given that none of his works explicitly refers to practices of satanic evocation. Crowley's atheism consists in the rejection of any God other than man. Indeed, in this sense he also criticizes some groups of

Satanists; they, venerating the devil as if he were a God, as a being external to man, do nothing but adopt the same Christian vision of the world. In other words, they would like to overwhelm Christianity, but in reality they end up emulating it.

"These are fools that men adore; both their Gods & their men are fools." (Alesiter Crowley, The Book of the Law)

Aleister Crowley was certainly an eclectic, eccentric and bizarre character. It is reasonable to think that he was mistakenly indicated as a Satanist because of his provocative behavior, outside the moral framework of the era in which he lived. He founded a religion, Thelema, still recognized worldwide, during his time in Cefalù. The path of Thelema implies the breaking down of all artificial inhibitions in order to free the essential self, accompanied by training in yoga, concentration and self-analysis. In 1912 Crowley took over the leadership of the Ordo Templi Orientis (O.T.O.), the Order of the Temple of the East, a religious organization which, in 1924, he remodeled around the concept of Thelema; today the O.T.O. it is the only organization, internationally extended, whose purpose is to teach and promote the doctrines and practices of the crowleyan philosophical and religious system[8]. The path to enlightenment is divided by degrees. To reach the seventh degree means to be ready for the "secret of secrets", that is sexual magic. In order to get there, the adept must first have learned to reject the sense of sin and restriction and have begun the search for his true will. To reach the eighth degree means to be ready for the "secret marriages between gods and men", which can be carried out through a self-sexual technique. Furthermore, the precepts of the eighth grade recommend not to live sexuality in a banal or casual way. The top of the O.T.O. system consists of the ninth degree. After a fasting period, the O.T.O. celebrates the "sacrifice of the Eucharist", which inserts a coitus at the center of a magical ritual, followed by the preparation of the famous "Elixir" (a mixture of the sexual secretions of man and woman) that is drunk. Crowley's religion attributes an enormous power to the Elixir, so much so that it is only possible to consume it upon reaching the last degree of the O.T.O.

"I am above you and in you. My ecstasy is in yours. My joy is to see your joy." (Alesiter Crowley, The Book of the Law)

Twentieth-century Satanism finds another protagonist in Maria de Naglowska. She frequented various Parisian esoteric circles, until she began to distinguish herself for not being a common occultist: she spoke willingly of the role of Satan and Lucifer, of the practices of sexual magic and undoubtedly defined her conferences as "satanic". In a short time she became known as "the priestess of Satan". Her doctrine was very complex and sophisticated. The members of her order, the Knights of the Golden Arrow, had to pass tests to climb the "satanic mountain", divided by degrees. In the first degree, called "street sweeper", the initiate had to purify himself from all the doctrines of the world and begin to study the fundamental precepts of the new doctrine. In the second degree, known as the "Liberated Hunter", the adept had to pass a test, consisting of sexually joining a woman, called "spiritual guide", without reaching orgasm. Along with the practice of seed assimilation, that of its retention is also widespread in the occult tradition. The third degree is that of the "Invisible Knight" and lasts a few years. This degree encompasses the knowledge of three religions, the Jewish one as the religion of the Father, the Christian one as the religion of the Son and the Satanic one as the religion of the Mother. In the study of the religion of the Son it is necessary to understand how the figure of Judah was fundamental in history, since if he had not betrayed Jesus, Good would have ended up prevailing and, therefore, there would be no balance between Good and Evil. To conquer the last degree, the adept must take an exam on the most complex part of de Naglowska's satanic doctrine, followed by a practical exam. The adept will first have to establish a relationship with a virgin priestess, because virginity is the greatest satanic virtue, and then let himself be hanged and saved just before the hanging becomes fatal. The ritual ends with sexual union with the virgin priestess and the practice of spermatophagia. De Naglowska's doctrine was not actually very successful in the years following her death, probably because of its excessive complexity. However, together with Crowley, it will be rediscovered by the wave of Satanists that will grow after the Second World War.

Let me be mad, then, by all means! mad with the madness of Absinthe, the wildest, most luxurious madness in the world! Vive la folie! Vive l'amour! Vive l'animalisme! Vive le Diable.
Marie Corelli, Wormwood: A Drama of Paris

Another noteworthy case is that of John Whiteside Parson, better known as Jack Parson. He was born in 1912 to a wealthy family from Pasadena, Los Angeles. Parson was both an occultist and a man of science, enough to be defined by Werner Von Braun: "the real father of the US space program"[9]. The importance of Parson lies in his role as a passage between initiatory magic and real Satanism. Introvigne writes: "With Parson we find ourselves on the eve of real contemporary Satanism"[10]. Parson was also part of the Ordo Templi Orientis, and there he met Aleister Crowley. Under the name of Belarion Armiluss Al Dajjal, he wrote several literary works, such as "Freedom is a Two Edged Sword", "The Book of Babalon", "The Book of Anti-Christ".

"We are one nation, one world ... We cannot suppress the freedom of our brothers without killing ourselves" (Jack Parson)

His spiritual testament is certainly "The Manifesto of the Antichrist" in which, as Introvigne writes: "he exposes a harsh anti-Christianity that coexists curiously with a feeling of respect for Jesus

Christ, who would not have been *Christian* and would have taught sexual liberation" [11].

1.5. Contemporary Satanism, from 1950 to today

"The Satanist realizes that man, and the action and reaction of the universe, is responsible for everything, and doesn't mislead himself into thinking that someone cares." (Anton LaVey)

If Aleister Crowley is the reference for classical Satanism, for contemporary Satanism we must quote Anton Szandor LaVey. Unlike Crowley, whose activity and thought remained more reserved and widespread only among the followers of the occult world, the Church of Satan and the name of Anton LaVey were in the public domain, spied on by the media and known also overseas. "LaVey's satanism is officially disapproved but in reality widely tolerated by the dominant culture which, for the first time, seems willing to accept the discourse - proposed by the first anthropologists and sociologists who study the phenomenon - which sees Satanism as a manifestation of its contradictions" (Introvigne 2010, p. 17). Together with Kenneth Anger, follower of Crowley, American screenwriter and director, LaVey founded the Church of Satan in San Francisco, California in 1966 ("Year One of Satan"). Thanks to Anger's connections in the world of Californian cinema, the success of the Church of Satan was assured. LaVey was soon nicknamed "the Pope of Satan". He wanted to be the personification of the Devil, he wandered with horns on his head and a tail attached to his body, while making the sign of the horns with his hands[12]. LaVey wanted his to be a real Church; in fact, since 1967, he began to celebrate weddings, baptisms and satanic funerals, attracting even more attention to himself.

"My manner of thinking, so you say, cannot be approved. Do you suppose I care? A poor fool indeed is he who adopts a manner of thinking for others!" (Marquis de Sade)

His most famous texts are "The Satanic Bible" (1969) and "The Satanic Rituals" (1972), which are certainly not lacking in the library of the modern Satanist; indeed they are probably the first two books he purchased. The Satanic Rituals is the demure version and contains internal satanic rituals for members of the Church of Satan. It is the manual for the black Mass of contemporary Satanists. By reversing the Catholic ritual, there are insults to Jesus Christ in all parts of the Mass (in Glory, in the Epistle, in the Gradual and in the Offertory) and the naked woman lying as an altar. There are two phases: that of desecration and that of consecration. In the first phase, a consecrated host is introduced into the vagina of the woman lying on the altar, who masturbates and is masturbated by the priest with the host itself until orgasm is reached. After the orgasm, the host is burned. In the second phase, however, it is the priest who masturbates until he reaches ejaculation. The ejaculation product is collected in a spoon and mixed with wine, and is consumed by those present. The reversal of the Catholic ritual, the insults to the Christian religion, the naked lying woman, the "Elixir of Life" (the sperm and the wine mixed) to drink have all already been mentioned previously. It is a fusion of Huysmans' literature and Aleister Crowley's doctrine of spermatophagia. How to interpret LaVey's Satanism? LaVey himself says that "Satan is a symbol, nothing more"[13]. His philosophy is in some ways similar to Crowley's. In fact, for LaVey man is the only God, and every man is solely responsible for his actions and his destiny. Unlike the other Satanist cults, in which Satan is a divinity, an external and superior entity to be served and worshiped during the Masses, for LaVey it is an internal force to man, which can achieve its objectives without asking for external intercessions. This message is basically common to all Satanist currents of thought: refusing control of one's life by third parties and living responsibly and autonomously leads to a fulfilled and free existence. Even the black Mass, then, does not serve to ask for the intercession of a divinity. In fact, "it is not a question of revering Satan as a real character but of staging a psychodrama in the most authentic sense, intended to free Christians and in particular Catholics from indoctrination passed through shock therapy" (Introvigne 2010, p 265).

"Satanism encourages its followers to indulge in their natural desires. Only by doing so can you be a completely satisfied person

with no frustrations which can be harmful to yourself and others around you. Therefore, the most simplified description of the Satanic belief is: indulgence instead of abstinence." (Anton LaVey)

Some of those who would like to become Satanists read LaVey's books and end up committing crimes believing they are following his teachings. In fact, LaVey has always kept pointing out that the Church of Satan is a peaceful and law-abiding organization, which does not tolerate animal or human sacrifices, nor the use of drugs. In 1975 the Church of Satan recorded a rift inside it; LaVey clashed with one of his most loyal collaborators, Michael Aquino, about managing the relationship between the Church of Satan and his followers, which had grown over the years. From 1975 onwards the faithful of a real Satanism, which believes in the existence of a real Satan, follow Aquino in his Temple of Set[14], which still survives today. Instead, esotericism enthusiasts, the curious of the macabre, the horror films, the myths about vampires and werewolves became the main followers of LaVey, who in part set aside his attention for "religious" themes. The case of "The Process" is different. This movement, whose full name is "The Process Church of the Final Judgment", has a different origin than modern cults, which refer to the Church of Satan. Its founders were Robert De Grimston Moore (1935) and Mary Ann Maclean (1931). The two met during a brief experience in Scientology[15]. They married in 1963 and in March 1966 they developed a magical-religious vision that required them to look for a sort of sacred place where they could experience the next stages of their spiritual journey. The two, together with twenty-five followers, left their London office and, after a series of mental visualizations and numerous travels, finally arrived in Mexico City, Yucatan. They settled in a place called Xtul ("terminus" in the Mayan language), where the members of the group had, according to their words, an encounter with God himself[16]. The sect acquired a hierarchical structure, at the top of which the Omega (the two founding spouses) stood out followed by other figures called prophets, priests and messengers. However, the group soon had to leave Mexico due to protests from some anti-sect movements. In 1966 the sect then returned to settle in London, and it is here that De Grimston transformed the initial doctrine. He had studied Jung's theories, especially the investigations of the psychologist on the dark side of the human being, and on the basis of these studies he enunciated the doctrine of the four divinities: Jehovah, Lucifer, Satan and Christ. The final goal of the path of human liberation would be the adoration of Christ, which can only be reached through the three previous divinities. The first step is to worship Satan. According to this doctrine, Satan would have already extended his influence to all mankind, who would therefore already be evil, and worshiping Satan would only amount to admitting it. Satan's purpose is twofold: on the one hand, he stimulates the overcoming of instinctive material passions and leads the human soul to freedom, towards a new dimension of existence; on the other hand, the Devil destroys all human morality, pushing man towards madness and violence. The dictates of the sect do not say to follow this second aspect of Satan to the end, but nevertheless prescribe to face it and accept it as a possibility. The sect therefore does not directly encourage crime, but the adept will, at this stage, experience all sorts of transgressions. An emissary, that is, a more expert member of the sect, will have the task of guiding the adept along this path. All divinities are closely related to each other, and each of them plays a specific role in this "quadrinity". The characters of these deities are expressed as follows:

• Jehovah: vengeful and angry, requires obedience, integrity and self-denial.

• Lucifer: not to be confused with Satan, he represents earthly happiness. From him come wealth and strength, love and peace, harmony and order.

• Satan: the god of darkness and transgression. He receives the souls of the dead and instigates the human being to walk the paths of instinct to the extreme.

• Christ: the emissary of the previous divinities, the last stage of the path of liberation. Christ realizes divine unity and leads man to the integration of his own self and to liberation.

The Process, like many other sects before it, also met a schism: Mary Ann Maclean and Robert De Grimston Moore divorced and, in 1974, Mary Ann led a group that eliminated all references to Lucifer and Satan. The original group instead remained under the leadership of De Grimston, who continued the previous journey. Today it has disappeared, while the Christian branch of the ex-wife has weakened more and more.

1.6. The great hunt for Satanists: the 80's and 90's of the 20th century

"When you're in hell, only a devil can point the way out."

(Joe Abercrombie, Half a King)

Over time, more and more people became interested in Satanism, giving rise to new sects and religious movements, to the point that the phenomenon began to worry public opinion. In the 1980s, the last great hunt for Satanists in history occurred, second only to the famous witch hunt of a few centuries earlier. Many young people moved away from family, school and work to devote themselves fully to the activities of these new religious movements. Families asked psychiatrists for help. In this perspective, secular anti-cult movements and religious anti-cult movements spread (Introvigne 2010, p. 310). The volume that started the whole secular anti - Satanist movement is "Michelle Remembers" from 1980, based on the work of the psychologist Lawrence Pazder and his patient Michelle Smith. Michelle was being treated by Dr. Pazder for a depression. At some point in the therapy, Michelle started talking like a little girl and telling of torture and violence she would be subjected to, orgies and human sacrifices she would witness. Thus it turns out that at the age of five her mother would consecrate her to the Devil, thus forcing her to attend a satanic ceremony. The book was a huge success until Michelle's father denied everything, saying that his late wife never cared about Satanism and would never let her daughter experience such violence. Also in 1980, the American Psychiatric Association included the Multiple Personality Disorder syndrome (MPD) in the DSM-III[17]. American and Canadian psychiatrists diagnosed MPD in very high quantities to patients who appeared to have suffered abuse, violence and torture on a satanic background during their childhood. There were so many diagnoses of MPD that the medical community started talking about an epidemic. Television, books and newspapers began to spread the testimonies of the «survivors», who told of the violence they had been victims of as children. Impressive numbers of "ritual" child abuse were reported, to the point that even the judicial authorities began to worry about it more and more. Given that abuse and violence against children are very serious episodes to be taken seriously, the scientific community began to wonder if there was really a satanic reference in these abuses, or if this was the effect of the mental manipulation acted by various therapists on children during the interviews. We know that children often have problems with "false memories", that their beliefs are easily manipulated and that they lie. In fact, even today, psychologists who have to deal with these delicate cases are advised to pay attention to "pseudo abuses", that is, stories of abuses that seem true, but which are, actually, erroneous beliefs elaborated on the basis of false interpretations of the reality that surrounds them, sometimes induced by their parents or, as in the case previously hypothesized, by the therapist. Another possibility relates to the fact that, in the dramatic context of child abuse, pedophiles use satanic symbols and references to impress and attract victims to themselves, without however being truly Satanists.

"We have never heard the devil's side of the story, God wrote all the book." (Anatole France)

The religious counter-Satanist movement, on the other hand, focused on the accusation against school textbooks, games, music, television and cinema, which would be guilty of starting in a hidden and perverse way not only to occultism, but even to real Satanism. In the 1990s, in the United States, there was a violent campaign against some school books believed to be responsible for telling children magic stories. Groups of Catholic fundamentalists fought to eliminate not only the books of Anton LaVey from public libraries, but also texts and great classics of literature where witches and magical rites appear. J. K. Rowling's "Harry Potter" novels became the scapegoat for this whole battle, as they taught that personal benefits could be gained with magic. Controversies regarding the literary saga still continue today: in 2019, in fact, a

Tennessee school removed the book from its shelves, as a local priest believed that the text could have induced readers to want to evoke evil spirits. The scapegoat for role-playing games is the famous "Dungeons and Dragons", because it is full of imaginative characters such as wizards, witches and goblins. And the music? As we know, music is a strong means of affiliation for young people, it creates a sense of belonging and identity, it is an instrument of expression, but also of rebellion. Heavy metal bands like Black Sabbath have repeatedly cited Satan in their songs. Then, in the 80s, two subgenres of heavy metal were created even more bloody in sounds and texts, namely death metal, which makes continuous morbid references to death and suicide, and black metal, in which there are attacks on Christianity and hymns to Satan. Black metal is certainly the metal current that comes closest to Satanism. This musical genre owes its name to Venom: the name "black", in fact, comes from the title of their second album, "Black Metal" (1982). The lyrics of their songs are violent and bloody, full of insults towards the Church and the Christian religion.

"If you can think of every cliché, that's us. The loud, the fast, the bombs, the black magic .... We are every cliché." (Abaddon to Ian Ravendale, Kerrang! September 1981)

The first followers of this genre, however, were harmless. They listened to songs, dressed in Gothic style, made up their faces in black and white, wore long hair and studded belts, but had no interest in committing satanic rites or crimes. Violence remained limited in the lyrics of the songs. Black metal was a marketing strategy rather than a real way of being. The teenagers, in order to challenge and scandalize their parents, bought the CDs of Venom, Celtic Frost, Mercyful Fate and dressed in leather and studs, because sex and swear words no longer caused a sensation. Indeed, some heavy metal groups and singers, such as Ozzy Osbourne (former member of Black Sabbath) and Judas Priest were sued in court by parents of suicidal teenagers, who held them responsible for the tragic deaths. Courts never accepted these parents' theses, as the incidence of suicidal teenagers who listened to satanic rock was the same as in the general population; therefore it was not possible to suppose that this kind of music instigated suicide, even if explicit reference was made in the texts. It was in the 1990s that things changed, with the emergence of "acid Satanism"[18] in which drug abuse, youthful unease and Satan's worship met. The typical scenario involves a group of young people reading some books about Satanism (almost always the texts of LaVey, easily available today); from here we move on to drug use and the improvisation of a satanic rite, up to the sacrifice of some animals. The use of drugs makes it easier to move on to more serious crimes, such as rape and murder. This is the so-called "acid Satanism". Although LaVey has always condemned both animal and human sacrifices and recommended compliance with the laws, it is easy for an unprepared teenager to misunderstand his doctrine and implement prevaricating behavior on the other, violence and rejection of moral and ethical norms. As easily understood, this type of Satanism is far from real Satanism. Sociologists call it "pseudo-Satanism", since there is no real devotion to the devil and any intention of creating a new religion is lacking. Rather, acid Satanism represents a way in which young people vent their frustrations and challenge the world of adults, using the strongest form of transgression they know: Satan. However, even if it is not true Satanism, it is probably the form that must frighten the most, due to its criminal potential. It is less controllable, and therefore more dangerous, than the official Churches of Satan. The 1990s saw the end of the great hunt for Satanists. Of all the stories of human sacrifices and murders reported by survivors and children, many turn out to be bogus and, in most alleged cases of murder, even corpses were missing. The anti-Satanists replied that the bodies were made to disappear in various ways, and that the sacrificed children did not appear to have disappeared as they were children born to women who gave birth to them purposely for the rituals, without reporting them to the registry office[19]. These answers are of little value, given that, in fact, even the most careful and organized criminal association would not be able to cover up crimes of this magnitude. It was two publications that decreed the end of this hunt, one by the sociologist Jean La Fontaine for the British government, and the other by the psychologist Gail S. Goodman for the National Center on Child Abuse and Neglect in the United States. "For the American report on twelve thousand reports of sexual abuse in the context of satanic group rituals, born of psychiatrists, social workers or police officers, not a single case could be supported by evidence" (Introvigne 2010, p. 365).

1.6.1. The Devils of the lower Modena

"I am quite sure I am more afraid of people who are themselves terrified of the devil than I am of the devil himself." (Santa Teresa de Jesús, The Life of Saint Teresa of Ávila by Hersel)

The case of the "Devils of the lower Modena" is emblematic of how often the Devil is seen even where he is not there, and how panic is the bearer of much more damage than any demon. We are in Italy, between 1997 and 1998, and it seemed that a sect, called "Devils of the lower Modena", organized satanic rites which included the abuse and murder of children. It all began with the denunciation of a child, which was soon followed by many others. Over twenty people were accused of being part of the sect, which allegedly sexually, physically and psychologically abused sixteen children, aged between zero and twelve, both within the walls of their houses and through satanic rites in the cemeteries in the area[20]. The sixteen children were permanently removed from their families; they were assigned to foster families and none of them ever returned home. However, the truth established that there were neither satanic rites nor much unless murders were committed, and it was also speculated that children's interrogation techniques led to these false memories being believed.[21][22][23][24][25] We must focus on how children were questioned (in particular for the use of the so-called "progressive disclosure" technique). The defendants' lawyers accused the social services of having influenced the children; investigations revealed footage of children's interrogations conducted by social workers:

"What did you feel when we brought you back to that square?" Asks the psychologist. "Joy," replies the little girl. "Are you sure? Think about it, maybe it was another emotion." "Joy!" "not a little bit of suffering too?" the girl nods. "In another video, a boy talks about sticking and drinking blood and, when asked what his mom was doing in the meantime, the boy replies that *She was washing the blood...* Is what I said okay?". In another he says "I killed at least five, but even more!"[26]

1.7. The acid Satanism of the 90's

- *"Are you a devil?"*

- *"I am a man,"* answered Father Brown gravely; *"and therefore have all devils in my heart." (G. K. Chesterton)*

After Anton LaVey's death on October 29, 1997, the Church of Satan began a new phase, initially under the guidance of the daughters of LaVey, Zeena and Karla, then under the aegis of his latest partner, Blanche Barton. Today the high priest is Peter H. Gilmore, flanked by his wife Peggy Nadramia. To date it is impossible to establish with certainty the actual number of followers of the Church of Satan, even if they are probably more than we can imagine. The fundamental difference from the early years of the Church founded by the "Black Pope" is free internet access. Today anyone, with a simple online search, can access the web page of the Church of Satan[27], can access forums where Satanism is talked about and collect any information they want to look for. Anyone can be a Satanist without being part of a sect or having ever attended a black Mass. Black metal also experienced a new phase. It originated in Norway, in a record store in Oslo, the Helvete (which means "hell" in Norwegian), and quickly spread to Scandinavia and Poland. The musicians of this second wave of black metal condemn the colleagues of the first wave and of other parallel genres, accusing them of not being true Satanists, of doing facade Satanism, useful only to sell records and concert tickets. True Satanism, according to these musicians, is synonymous with death, destruction and terror. The true follower must terrify anyone who approaches him, sowing panic. Christianity is comparable to the worst of epidemics, to a plague, a spiritual infection that must be eradicated to make room for Satan, the only one that can free us from the prison to which the Church, Jesus and God condemn us. What they propose, unlike other groups of Satanists, it is the transition to action. The goal is not to spread the satanic cult by speaking, but by acting and spreading chaos and violence. In the early 1990s, numerous churches and religious buildings were burned in Norway, there were numerous stabbings and rivals who did not commit suicide in Satan's name by choice were killed. It was a period that did not last long and ended up extinguishing itself, although some events unfortunately inspired groups of teenagers elsewhere, as the Italian case of the Beasts of Satan confirms us.

"The truth is, the Devil's job is easy." (Tyler Edwards, Zombie Church: Breathing Life Back Into the Body of Christ)

The groups of Satanists in Italy, according to the Report on Satanism in Italy[28], which collected all the complaints received by Telefono Antiplagio from 1994 to 2007, would be more than 500: 236 in northern Italy, 122 in central Italy, 92 in southern Italy and 58 in the islands. Of all these sects, the most famous are "The Children of Satan" and "The Beasts of Satan". The Children of Satan, once known as Luciferian Children of Satan (B. S. L.), are a satanic sect that grew up in the city of Bologna; one of the most influential characters is certainly Marco Dimitri. The latter approached Satanism by reading Crowley; he always defined himself as a Satanist and began to perform satanic rites between

Bologna, Forlì, Rimini and Riccione. Crowley's influence is evident in the "Red Masses" which are celebrated in addition to the Black Masses; they consist of large orgies where sexual intercourse, both straight and homosexual, is consumed. The "Infernal Gospel" is the sacred text of the Children of Satan, which describes for the most part sexual intercourse of various kinds and orgiastic rites. The church where the masses are held, black and red, is adorned with large dark drapes, skulls, statues of the Devil and frightening masks. The Children of Satan[29] are not believers or religious, but pure and simple rationalists. They specify it whenever they can, so that they are never mistaken for devil worshipers. Their devotion seems instead entirely concentrated on official science, which becomes the only God who can be believed always, in any case. The Children of Satan are an organization that offers a full range of services to their followers, divided into fourteen different categories of rituals. Among these are heterosexual and homosexual marriages, between two or more people (man-man-woman, woman-woman-man, woman-woman-woman, man-man-man) and incestuous. Since marriage exists, there is also a divorce rite. For Catholics and adherents to other religions there is also a "ceremony of annulment of baptismal rites of any cult" to begin satanic baptism. Between 1989 and 1992 the Carabinieri began to investigate the activities of the Children of Satan. In 1992 they broke into a rite, but the investigation ended without any conviction. In 1996, however, more serious allegations of carnal violence against a minor girl and a child emerged, as well as rumors of human sacrifices. Together with two accomplices, Dimitri was arrested and later acquitted. In the Italian scene, the Beasts of Satan also stand out. We know they were a group of young people who decided to form a satanic sect, who listened to black metal music and used drugs. They were young people without ideas, with no enthusiasm, no imagination, impoverished by unhappy family stories, bored by the present and afraid of the future, unable to get excited about simple things. Satan gave them an answer. Their profile faithfully reflects that of acid Satanism. Italy has, perhaps, the primacy of murders caused by acid Satanism. Before the Beasts of Satan, there was another case in Chiavenna (in the Province of Sondrio), on the evening of June 6, 2000. Sister Maria Laura Mainetti was killed by three underage girls in a park near the convent where she lived. During the interrogation, the three girls said that the nun had been chosen because she was a symbol of purity. They used to meet and practice some improvised satanic rite, until the decision to make a human sacrifice. Next to the victim's body they left the symbol of a five-pointed star with three numbers six written on it. A month before carrying out the crime, they made a pact of blood: they cut themselves and collected their blood in a glass with water, then drunk in turn. Their Satanism was of a homemade type, without any reference to organized groups, a Satanism read on books and seen on television, just like the Satanism of almost all acidic groups.

"... you cannot shake hands with the Devil and not get sulfur on

your sleeve." (Nancy A. Collins)

What should frighten us about these groups is the fact that they are uncontrollable, that they can arise at any moment and that it is the groups that are guilty of the most serious crimes. Organized adult Satanism, in fact, was not born with the intent to commit crimes; it is not exactly dangerous. However, there is not only acid and organized Satanism. We know that today there are many types of sects and many types of Satanism, all very different from each other, on which it is possible to make reflections and classifications.

1.8 Categorizations

"Should we blame the devil for our sins? I think no, absolutely no." (Edward Marion)

Massimo Introvigne, in his book "The Magician's Hat" (1995), theorized a categorization of Satanism to which reference is still made:

• rationalist Satanism;

• occultist Satanism;

• acid Satanism;

• luciferism.

Rationalist Satanism refers to the thought of Anton LaVey; it does not believe in the existence of the devil and considers Satan the symbol of transgression, pleasure, reason and nonconformity. It is therefore an "atheist religion", which enhances the cult of reason and uses the symbol of the Devil as an extreme antithesis of the dominant culture, permeated by religion and Catholic morality. Occultist Satanism instead refers to the doctrine of Michael A. Aquino and the Temple of Set. In this case Satan is considered no longer a symbol, but a real divinity, a living and real presence. The biblical devil is venerated through the rite of the black mass, which is nothing other than the inversion of the Catholic rite, where hatred for the Christian God and love for Satan is proclaimed. Acid Satanism is what was mentioned in the previous paragraph. An unorganized group of teenagers who share a taste for the same music (heavy metal) and for drugs. They are not real Satanists, and Satan becomes the excuse for taking drugs and scandalizing adults. Satanic books and magazines are read, rudimentary rites are performed in which animals are sacrificed and cemeteries are profaned. Crimes are committed, which as we have mentioned go as far as murder and rape. Luciferism is a current that venerates Lucifer, the angel of the Bible fallen from heaven, but without considering him evil; on the contrary, it is seen as a positive figure. Lucifer is revered as a principle of good in opposition to the god of evil and creator of the world: the Demiurge[30]. Francesco Barresi (2006), sociologist and criminologist, proposes another categorization based instead on the behavioral-motivational mode of the Satanist, that is, in relation to the group in which he is and the external environment.

• religious Satanism, in which the adept is devoted to Satan and believes that it exists as a real entity;

• ludic Satanism, in which the adept performs rituals for fun, without really knowing or believing in Satanism;

• sexual Satanism, which is linked to a purely physical approach;

• schizophrenic Satanism, in which the adept suffers from psychotic disorders and has a distorted view of reality.

Barresi (2006, p. 163) also classifies adepts into three categories:

• solitary Satanists, individuals who practice and profess their religion in an intimate and private way, without joining any satanic group. The loners can be: "real loners", truly lonely individuals, without social networks, who do not profess their beliefs externally; "Loner delusional schizophrenic and hebephrenic", psychotic individuals who because of illness believe they are truly subjected to a hellish divinity; "Ludical loners", young individuals who play Satanists, improvising rites in their own room; "Egotic solitaries", individuals who despise the community and practice a Satanism centered on their personal and sexual growth; "Professional loners", individuals who work as magicians or fortune tellers;

• intermediate Satanists, that is, those who are interested in Satanism and are moving from individual Satanism to social Satanism;

• group Satanists, that is, those who profess their belief in sharing with other people. In this group there are five sub-categories of Satanists: the "charismatics", who often become the leaders of the group; the "sexual paraphilics", who feel legitimized to give vent to their paraphilias[31] and sexual perversions within the group; the "egotics", who profess a derogatory belief towards society; the "drug addicts" who participate in the group to use drugs that are given during the rites; the "ludics", who approach Satanism for fun and fun, to try orgies, to try new drugs.

In conclusion, we can say that pure Satanism is nothing but the metaphor and mirror of modernity, to which all veils are removed. Through Satanism, the modern individual can see himself in the mirror. The strong that prevails over the weak, the search for power and wealth, sex for its own sake; is it not what the human being wants under the mask? Satanism has the dirty task of removing this mask, and showing us the world and man for who they are, without superstructures and without veils.

"I saw the devil today and he looked a lot like me" (Five Finger Death Punch)

The cycle history of Satanism will probably continue in the future as well, because society will always go through moments of crisis, and the human being will always be in search of the truth, even the most uncomfortable one.

CHAPTER TWO

RELIGIOUS SECTS AND ADOLESCENCE

"When you know what a man wants you know who he is, and how to move him."(George R.R. Martin, A Storm of Swords)

We are what we have. It is television, newspapers, cinema and the internet that decide who we should be, who decides who will be successful and who will not. We can be successful people only if we comply with their dictates, only if we follow their rules, only if we buy their products. That product is absolutely necessary because it is fashionable. Regardless of what we need, we must immediately buy it. We are no longer able to recognize our real needs: the emotional, relational needs, the need to be bored, to waste time, to sleep, the need to listen to us, to be with ourselves. It is a continuous race. We live in a society that forces us to success, to fame, and tells us that whoever stops is lost. But why? This frantic race to get us always different and more intense experiences creates a sort of emotional anesthesia. We are no longer able to get excited about simple things, to appreciate the different, to feel curiosity, to discover new things. We are losing the ability to critically evaluate what surrounds us. Television and the internet are our means of contact with the world, and they show us exasperated, harsh, raw and violent images, which, however, do not impress us much. Who is still shocked to hear about death and war? The news now bores us. There is a serious crisis in culture, institutions, thinking, values, projects, roles and identities. Everything today is directly connected to money. We acquire value as people if we produce a lot and in a short time. Those who are unable to produce are worthless; it is no coincidence that we continually forget the needs and existence of the elderly and disabled: they do not produce, do not work, do not serve, have no value, and yet they exist. Social ties are in crisis. Teenagers can only establish relationships if mediated by the use of mobile phones and computers. Sometimes they also talk to their parents via messages, and parents have adapted to this system. Face-to-face relationships have become difficult and tiring. The family is changing[32], nuclear families (married couple and any legitimate children) are less and less frequent and single-parent or reconstituted families are more and more frequent. The rate of separations and divorces is steadily increasing. We live in the era of communication but we find it increasingly difficult to establish stable, serene and sincere relationships. Affective relationships enter into crisis when the first phase of falling in love ends, and the other person becomes a source of anxiety and fear. Fear of losing your identity, your goals, your projects. This anxiety and this fear in emotional relationships have their origin in the narcissism towards which we are driven by the context in which we live: self-affirmation and success at all costs, attention to oneself and one's needs, alienation and the depersonalization of others. The search for the meaning of life is increasingly entrusted to the individual and attention to oneself has put in crisis values such as trust, solidarity and reciprocity. We need others, but we don't know how much. Experiencing strong emotions reminds us that we are alive, we are looking for increasingly intense and always different emotions to feel alive, happy.

"Civilization is drugs, alcohol, engines of war, prostitution, machines and machine slaves, low wages, bad food, bad taste, prisons, reformatories, lunatic asylums, divorce, perversion, brutal sports, suicides, infanticide, cinema, quackery, demagogy , strikes, lockouts, revolutions, putsches, colonization, electric chairs, guillotines, sabotage, floods, famine, disease, gangsters, money barons, horse racing, fashion shows, poodle dogs, chow dogs, Siamese cats, condoms, peccaries, syphilis, gonorrhea, insanity, neuroses, etc. etc." (Henry Miller)

"Happiness" therefore becomes the key word of the modern world, the emblem of modernity. The pursuit of happiness opens the door to a series of characters of dubious morality who promise and sell happiness to people. The insecurity, confusion and precariousness that modern man experiences push him to take on any bait in order to suddenly feel happy. Hundreds of pseudo-religious groups exploit this mood by bringing people closer to new cults modeled ad hoc, promising them the much desired happiness. Of these, the most captivating are certainly the esoteric groups, which make use of magic, which man has always used to try to have control over external events and phenomena that he could not understand. *"The fascination of the occult therefore lies in the illusion of being able to directly influence one's condition, modifying it in relation to one's needs, of having power over oneself and others rather than feeling at the mercy of external events to find a solution to own problems"* (Cantelmi, Cacace 2007, p. 20). Sects, congregations and pseudo-religious associations find themselves in the right place and at the right time, in a fragmented society that generates equally fragmented and frightened individuals. These groups offer a vision of the world that is already widespread and known, to which they add new and different elements that can give a religious explanation to the discomfort and evil of society, without however straying too far from the majority culture. They appeal to a few followers and remain rather small groups, so that members can feel important, bind and become entangled faster, without feeling anonymous, abandoned and lost as in external society. Several studies have verified that the people who are interested and who end up joining a sect are people who have experienced or collected a series of negative experiences on an individual level, such as problems during the primary socialization phase, periods of constant change, failures on a relational or work level. Joining a sect is a way to claim, not to give up, to try to react to one's own unease (ibid, p. 27).

"Unhappy people can be very dangerous, don't forget that."

(S.E. Lynes)

A very strong mechanism of cohesion and socialization is generated within the sect. Finally we feel like someone, finally we feel part of something, we feel important. Being part of a sect increases self-esteem and decreases anxiety. You have the feeling that you can control any aspect of your life and thus put an end to your frustration. Entering a sect is very easy, but leaving it is not, precisely for these reasons. Losing the support and references that have given meaning to one's being in the world, that have given importance and attention to one's own person, that have generated psychological and sometimes even physical well-being, is difficult for a fragile ego.

1. What is a sect

"A sect, incidentally, is a religion with no political power." (Thomas Wolfe)

The term "sect" can have two interpretations depending on the etymological root attributed to it. Sect can derive from the Latin "secta", from the verb "secor", which means "to follow, go behind", or it can also derive from the verb seco, which means "to cut, separate, disconnect". So if the first derivation is adopted a sect is a group of people who decide to follow a particular doctrine or leader. In the second derivation, however, a sect is a group of people who have separated themselves from a majority doctrine. The groups labeled as sects have always been groups of a religious nature, which have separated and opposed to official religions, creating new principles and new dogmas, adopting their own different vision of the world and their own lifestyle. It is a phenomenon that began to grow in the early 1900s, coinciding with the processes of schooling and secularization, whereby religious institutions began to lose credibility and social significance. In particular, in the 1960s and 1970s, youth movements started a process of globalization and rediscovery of spirituality. In this climate dozens of new sects and religious movements have arisen, precisely to depart from the strict and unfulfilling conformism of previous years. In the last few years a negative connotation has been associated with the term sect; this is because religious groups have always frightened the majority, because they have always been very closed to the outside and shrouded in mystery. Getting in is easy, it's a choice. We choose not to follow the official doctrine anymore to follow a minority that seems to respond better to our needs and our questions. Generally all sects have a hierarchical and pyramidal structure that sees a "charismatic leader" at the head, who is almost always the founder of the sect. Below him, depending on how the group has decided to organize itself, there may be celebrants, ministers, older brothers and sisters, main members. The older sisters and brothers have the task of instructing the recruiters, who in turn have the task of looking for new followers. The main members, on the other hand, tend to deal with the new followers. The latter must always support a path of initiation and personal transformation which, in most cases, is not devoid of forms of psychological conditioning and mental manipulation (Cantelmi, Cacace 2007, p. 30).

2. Young people at risk

"Every rebellion implies some kind of unity." (Albert Camus)

Adolescence and rebellion are often synonymous. During adolescence, rebellion is a positive symptom of growth. Refusing, reacting, challenging and rebelling against the adult world is necessary so that the young person can build his own identity and no longer be dependent on that of his parents. The adult world is completely rejected in all its aspects: the way of dressing, the way of speaking, eating, thinking. How many times do we see scenes in malls where a mother shows her daughter a T-shirt and she replies that it "sucks"? As soon as we enter adolescence, we start saying a lot of bad words, or inventing new ones that parents don't know. We want to reject the adult world, reject the limits within which the life of one's parents takes place, overcome them. Sex no longer scandalizes so much, and neither do drugs. But Satanism is still frightening. Young people who choose Satanism experience the same exact discomfort and the same identical frustration as all other teenagers, but choose, as a solution, a doctrine that has little to teach from an ethical, moral and religious point of view. Still, Satanism has its charm because mysterious things always attract a little more. The occult fascinates, as does magic. The idea of being able to use magic makes one feel special, gives a sense of power and omnipotence. The adolescent is also interested in Satanism because he has the opportunity to use drugs and make sex easy, without having to look elsewhere. By accepting to be part of a group that is not well viewed by the outside world, which rather frightens, and even committing small crimes (for example thefts to buy drugs, threatening an external person for favors), all you do is challenge the authority, the system, society and adults. Why not choose Satanism? It promises power, control, success, gives the idea of eing invincible and special, which is basically all that today's society pushes us to, that is to be successful people and have everything we want. It is difficult to be a teenager today: you have to challenge an adult world that is in crisis itself.

The young man, who needs to face a solid cultural system, finds instability, emptiness and fragmentation. While in the past young people clashed with a firm family and a steady social world, and from the conflict with it they could build an adult identity with equally strong values and roles, today this is no longer possible, and teenagers struggle to understand the world, bombarded by the alexithymic messages of the media. Teenagers most at risk are those who have a conflictual relationship with their parents, lonely, poorly communicative, who do not feel accepted by the peer group or have difficulty socializing, who have low self-esteem and are particularly insecure. For them, Satanism becomes the ideal solution to overcome the feelings of inadequacy and weakness. Cantelmi and Cacace (2007, p. 118) have listed a number of signs that should cause parents concern:

• sudden depression of mood;

• disinterest in school;

• decreased ability to concentrate;

• restlessness, aggression, sudden changes in mood;

• hostile rebellion;

• tendency to loneliness;

• sudden drop in school performance;

• changing interests and regular friends;

• interest in mythology, magic, rituals and symbolism;

• interest in the contents of violent, bloody occult;

• attraction for what is mysterious;

• excessive refusal of one's parents' religious values.

Obviously, in order to notice these warning signs and intervene accordingly, it is essential that parents talk and dialogue with their children, that they dedicate a lot of time to them and that they share the experience of growth with them. Give it a space that is above all emotional and psychic, in which they can feel heard and understood. Talk a lot, give advice, discuss, listen, show attention to their problems and interests, so that they always feel welcome and free to share their thoughts and anxieties. "Since no teenager takes refuge in extreme behavior without having first manifested his suffering in some way, if this type of relationship is established, it will be easier for parents to identify the inconveniences of their children, modify their wrong paths and do so that they feel less alone in their moments of difficulty" (ibid, p. 120)

3. Culture and criminogenesis

"Paradise is neither a moment nor a place; it is a condition. So when the lover calls to his or her beloved to come into the garden, it is, in the final implication, a summons to overcome to human condition." (Richard Cavendish, The Tarot)

Inadvertently, precisely because we are used to it, we are surrounded by references to esotericism, to the occult, to the magic, whether white or black, witchcraft, paganism and, why not, Satanism. Books, magazines, television, music, the web and cinema talk about it.

3.1 Books

The number of books dedicated to the new religious movements is constantly growing, so much so that there are more and more libraries dedicated only to this kind of texts. The occult is fascinating, teenagers often begin to be interested in it by reading novels focusing on the events of small religious sects, witchcraft or the use of magic. They are very cheap and easily available novels. Sometimes they are so engaging that they are used as an example by small groups of young people to define their religious purposes, the names, objectives and powers of individual members. The groups of neo-Satanists are inspired by texts of various kinds, sometimes also by school books and the works of great classics of literature (Carducci, Baudelaire, Milton) in which the figure of Satan appears, from comics, from videogames and role-playing games. As mentioned in the first chapter, the most popular book among all those who decide to seriously devote themselves to Satanism is Anton Sznador LaVey's "The Satanic Bible". Other widely used books are "The Satanic Rituals", also by LaVey, the "Malleus Maleficarum" by H. Kramer and J. Sprenger, the most famous texts by Aleister Crowley, such as "Magick" and "The Book of the Law", and the most famous black magic text , "The Black Arts" by Richard Cavendish. For those who decide to be a Satanist, the most important book of all is perhaps the Book of Darkness (Barresi 2006), which is nothing more than their own personal diary, in which to collect the rituals performed, the magic formulas, the rules of their sect. The Book of Darkness is personalized by every Satanist, sometimes it is written the other way round to make it encrypted, jealously guarded, decorated and covered with magical powers.

3.2 Objects

There are also criminogenic objects, without which it is not possible to participate in satanic rites. According to what is described in LaVey's Satanic Bible, to participate in satanic rites it is essential to wear a tunic with a hood, black or blood red or purple, handmade by each owner; it must be worn without any other garment. Depending on how organized the groups of Satanists are, they will need isolated places to meet, an altar (which often consists of a mattress), candles, consecrated hosts to desacralize and everything necessary for their rites. Sado-masochist satanic groups, for example, will need for their rituals - which consist of large organized orgies - latex suits, whips, collars, masks, sex toys, chains and studs.

"The belief in a supernatural source of evil is not necessary; men alone are quite capable of every wickedness." (Joseph Conrad)

3.3 Music

Music is one of the most powerful means of expression and aggregation for young people. Through music it is possible to communicate and share. Black and death metal music, if listened to by young people already alienated, frustrated and marginalized, does nothing but push them towards anti-social conduct. It conveys content that is contrary to socially shared and adaptive values: it communicates violence, selfishness, rebellion, aggression, abuse of power and apathy. In addition, it brings them closer to the world of acid Satanism, which we know is very dangerous. Beyond the satanic rock of the 80s and 90s, which was mentioned in the first chapter, today the music that is used by satanic groups is mostly electronic music. Electronic music has sounds capable of stimulating certain areas of the cerebral cortex that release endorphins. It is capable of altering the listener's state of consciousness, even more if under the influence of drugs. Some types of electronic music, such as techno, have a syncopated rhythm that imitates the heartbeat and very low tones and vibrations, which are listened to at a very high volume, so that they reverberate in the body and make the internal organs vibrate, especially those in the pelvic area. They are a natural aphrodisiac. In fact, these genres of music are listened to during the orgiastic phases of satanic rites, they help to let go and get completely lost. Many electronic artists, often for market needs, accompany their music with idolizing texts Satan and other evil demons.

3.4 Cinema and television

Once, in the western world, cinema and television were means of communication reserved only to that part of the population that could afford them, while today they have a universal diffusion. It is difficult not to find a TV in a house, and if it happens it is because of a choice, not because of economic impossibility. Thanks to the web, then, you can stream all the films you want. Needless to say, how many films have been made with reference to the Demon or the witches, and more generally how many horror films are full of violent and bloody scenes. In this kind of film, evil is often not manifest, but remains suspended and furtive. It creeps into the mind of the viewer, who ends up wanting it, imagining it and wanting to see its appearance. Evil is, in the end, mocking and victorious. Television is even more dangerous than cinema, since it offers us hidden contents without us having chosen them. The programming is full of allusions and occult practices, spells, reincarnations, magic and supernatural forces. The magical world that is presented is often an a-problematic world, where magic makes it possible to solve all daily problems. The programs that are broadcast today have an ethical content different from the fairy tales that were read to us as children. Good and evil no longer have clear boundaries, on the contrary, today the outlines are clearly blurred. The programs presented to the little ones present a relativistic conception of good and evil: there is a neutral force that can be used for both good and evil purposes.

"In many cases, it is very hard to fix the bounds of Good and Evil, because these part, as Day and Night, which are separated by Twilight." (Benjamin Whichcote)

Think of the TV series «Charmed», which has important contents from a criminogenic point of view. The three Witches are ordinary people, who live the same everyday world as all of us, but with magical powers. It is white magic, because the three Witches fight against evil. We see continuous spells that can change the fate of the protagonists, and magic eventually takes on a positive value. However, for the three girls to continue using magic, they must necessarily move away from their social relationships. They cannot have friends for fear that they will discover their secret; in the same way, they never see their family, they work for short periods and they don't go to school. That is, they live in real social isolation. Maybe we don't realize it immediately, but the impact and the suggestion that this TV series and other TV programs can have on younger people is not to be underestimated. The influence of the occult in today's television and cinema exists, and it is certainly very subtle and penetrating. Young people, without knowing it, undergo important criminogenic influences. Furthermore, being constantly exposed to strong, raw and violent images, albeit simulated and unreal, generates an emotional anesthesia in the adolescent that makes him unable to react in the face of violent or criminal episodes in real life.

4. Becoming a Satanist: mental manipulation

"- You are a manipulator.

- I like to think of myself more as an outcome engineer. "

(J.R. Ward, Lover Eternal)

Joining a satanic religious sect inevitably means undergoing a process of mental manipulation. All members of the sect, from newly-elected to leaders, undergo this process. Mental manipulation is possible in a situation where the relationship is asymmetrical: there must be one person with greater power than the others. Thanks to his position of power, the leader is able to exploit the victim's identity for his own purposes, threatening his integrity and autonomy, and making him almost totally dependent on himself and his will. The identity of each individual is a sum of beliefs, experiences, emotions and beliefs that derive from one's life path. Through the path of mental manipulation it is possible to "overwrite" a new group identity, which responds to the needs of the sect. Adepts undergo a precise technique of mental manipulation, which can be divided into five phases (Barresi 2006, p. 95):

• recruitment;

• starting up the doctrine;

• rooting in the group;

• removal from society and isolation;

• strengthening of the doctrine.

4.1 Recruitment

"Belief can be manipulated. Only knowledge is dangerous."

(Frank Herbert)

The group members charged with proselytizing never turn to a stranger disinterestedly: their goal is always to attract someone to their own sect. Since the first contact, the victim begins to suffer an initial emotional disorientation: it is made to fall in contradiction about what his beliefs and beliefs are, he is shown how his happiness is fictitious because subjugated by an infinite series of moral norms and cultural influences of this declining society. Failing to fight back, the victim is at fault and is often persuaded to be present at a first sectarian meeting. Once entered the sect, the person finds himself immersed in an artificial world made of happiness, warm and welcoming atmospheres and finds a harmonious and friendly group, which almost does not seem to be part of this world. The needs to feel part of something and to feel safe are immediately satisfied. The sectarian group is the answer to all problems. Within the sect, the new adept is approached by the elders of the group, who tell him how much their life has changed for the better, how they lived in the illusion of being happy and how much they really are now, thanks to this path of liberation and conversion that led them to discover the truth and give meaning to their lives. A recruiting technique widely used within satanic sects, given the extreme importance that sex has within these sects, is flirty fishing: some members of the sect have the task of seducing members of the opposite sex by flirting , and also have the task of drawing up a weekly report in which they communicate how many new followers they have managed to recruit.

4.2 Initiation to doctrine

"If you are an approval addict, your behavior is as easy to control as that of any other junkie. All a manipulator need do is a simple two-step process: Give you what you crave, and then threaten to take it away. Every drug dealer in the world plays this game." (Harriet B. Braiker, Who's Pulling Your Strings? How to Break the Cycle of Manipulation and Regain Control of Your Life)

Once part of the group, the adept is indoctrinated. He must read books, watch videos, attend meetings, seminars, listen to the leader or senior members. In the first phase of indoctrination, which is administered in small doses, the neophyte undergoes the so-called "love bomb": he is filled with affection, compliments and affective gratifications. Even his agenda is filled with commitments. All this affection and all this time spent together with the other members of the sect prevents the individual from reflecting critically on the doctrine that they are inculcating. He experiences a confusing state that leads him to suggest himself: the desire to remain part of the group and the desire to find this promised truth lead him not to build a critical knowledge. He doesn't care if his friends or family don't believe it, if there are pessimists and skeptics who mock him. He wants to go all the way because he has found a world where everyone loves him and protects him, and where he knows he will always be happy. In the second phase of indoctrination, after the adept's will has been completely subdued, the chief and senior members implement a strategy based on affective frustration. The objectives that the follower must achieve are moved higher and higher, so as to generate in him a series of disappointments, to which the group turns its back. The reaction that is generated in the adept is that of dependence: he will lose self-confidence and will be led to react by participating even more frequently and intensely in the group's activities and ideology. It is clear, for those who know it, that within this type of group the same dynamics are created and therefore the same symptoms of Stockholm Syndrome occur, in which an individual who is in a condition of dependence on another (for example, hostage and kidnapper), the natural feeling of resentment and contempt mutates in a feeling of affection and admiration, precisely because of the dependence of which he remains a victim. The new member can overcome frustration and disappointment only by adopting a new sect identity, which must inevitably replace his own. His cultural, critical, experiential background is deconstructed and restructured in a way more suited to the needs of the group.

4.3 Rooting in the group

"Welcome to the human race. Nobody controls his own life, Ender. The best you can do is choose to fill the roles given you by good people, by people who love you." (Orson Scott Card - *Ender's Game*)

We are in the most delicate phase. At this point the adept is completely inserted in the sect, the good times when he was pampered and guided step by step in the indoctrination are over. Now he is completely immersed in the hard and frenetic daily life of the sect, between missionary activities, work in the center, the procurement of money and the continuous rituals. He is placed in an uninterrupted work schedule, so that he does not have time for individual needs. He must change all his life habits and devote all his energies to respond to the group's requests. Sometimes the group prescribes members to deprive themselves of sleep, to fast or to follow strict diets. This way, the person experiences a psycho-physical condition of weakness, which does not allow him to question himself critically about what is happening to him or about the cult he is so fervently trusting. The psychological pressure exerted by the leader and the group increases more and more, and when the individual member fails to meet the needs of the group he is humiliated and, at times, punished. To uncertainty, inadequacy and the feeling of not feeling up to it, the adept responds by continuing to adapt and submit, increasing his commitment and discipline. His will is broken and subjugated to sectarian needs. It's not just a losing game, though. As compensation for all frustrations, members are guaranteed security: they no longer have daily worries, the sect takes care of all their problems, even those for the future and for what they left outside the sect, in an apparent climate of a-problematicity. Another very effective strategy for making neophytes root in the group is to engage them in missionary activities and to recruit new followers. Having to convince strangers of the positive effects and truth of their doctrine, they must first of all believe it themselves. Without realizing it, the members manipulate and condition their own conscience. Giulio Perrotta (2016) lists a series of behaviors implemented by the leaders of the satanic sects to manipulate the mind of the adepts:

a) Isolation. Getting people away from social support increases their psychological dependence on the leader;

b) Manipulation of perception. It can be implemented through the lack of light or excess lighting, or through particular types of diet. It induces to fix the attention on the present problems and an increases the introspective activity. It can also be used as a punishment for disobedience;

c) Induction of physical weakness. By means of sleep deprivation, poor diet, physical hyperactivity, it aims to weaken the mental and physical capacity to resist;

d) Threats. They generate anxiety and despair, much more than the action itself;

e) Occasional indulgences. They are sporadic favors and rewards, which prevent the individual from adapting to deprivation;

f) Degradation. These are humiliating conditions in which the individual is forced to stay (for example the impediment to intimate hygiene), which lead to a decrease in self-esteem and an increase in awe;

g) Trivial requests. They aim to develop the habit of obedience;

h) Hyperventilation. The adept must shout or chant aloud phrases or slogans with deep exhalation, passing large volumes of air inside and outside the lungs; in this way a phenomenon known as "respiratory alkalosis" is generated, which can also cause fainting. After shouting for a long time, people have very slow, too poor breathing to compensate for previous respiratory excesses and restore a chemical balance of the blood. The person feels weak, exhausted, aware of having lived a dramatic and upsetting experience.

There is no doubt, in short, that mental manipulation is the ideal tool for obtaining the psychological control of an individual, even pushing him to commit crimes that, on a conscious level, he probably would never have committed.

4.4 Removal from society and isolation

"One of the characteristics of sects is that they judge all other believers to be lost. What they claim, in effect is Unless you agree with me on all issues that I define as essential, you cannot be saved." (Flavil R. Yeakley Jr., Why They Left: Listening to Those Who Have Left Churches of Christ)

Once the follower has managed to resist and take root in the sectarian group, it is possible to continue the manipulation by moving him away from society and its past. The isolation pursues the aim of shielding the members from all the unpleasant influences of the outside world, so as to continue to make them available without reservations for the purposes of the sect. In this phase, the members of the group denigrate all the emotional relationships that the individual lives outside and all the values sent to him by society. He is absolutely forbidden to talk about the sect with relatives and friends (who, say the leaders of the sect, would not understand or hinder the new life of the adept). All the life experiences that the subject lived before joining the cult are devalued, especially on an emotional level, since they were lived within an aimless, meaningless existence. Only the experiences conducted within the sect make sense, have emotional value and deserve attention and emotional participation.

4.5 Strengthening the doctrine

"All control, in essence, is about who controls the truth." (Joseph Rain, The Unfinished Book About Who We Are)

In the fifth and final phase it is mainly a question of refining the mechanisms of dependence, of completing the control of conscience and of strengthening the identity of a sect. This is possible by continuing the rituals and indoctrination, even of elderly members, at an almost exhausting rate. However, the sect wants to avoid the resurface of the individual consciousness, and doubts about the life that is being conducted along with it. Insulation must also be kept under control. In some sects there is even a total control of information. Members are completely reduced or banned from the consumption of the media, all their exchanges with the external environment are controlled, forbidding phone calls and messages to their family members, (ex) friends or other external people. Leaving the sect is difficult, because through "involvement in increasingly transgressive rituals, which make him an accomplice and author of immoral or illegal practices, psychological control is constantly strengthened, to guarantee the total loyalty of the adept to the sect" (Cantelmi, Cacace 2007, p.

83). It is a fact that, however, some members sometimes manage to leave the sect. For them, the journey back to reality is very painful, and sometimes serious mental disorders arise. The original personal identity is not eliminated, as mentioned at the beginning of the paragraph, but is "overwritten", so the memories, emotions and perceptions of life can slowly resurface. However, this is a difficult path, so it is advisable to be accompanied by an expert.

"You may feel scared when starting again. Pull out your bravery and blaze a new life." (Tracy A Malone)

In the fifth edition of the DSM, «Dissociative disorder with other specification» was introduced, where the symptoms of dissociative disorder remain (manifestations of anxiety, phobias, panic attacks, eating disorders, sexual dysfunctions, feeling of unreality, estrangement from one's own self, perception of the environment, of people, family and non-familiar, as if they were unknown, doubts and identity loss), in relation to which the Manual also introduced "Identity disturbance due to prolonged and intense coercive persuasion". This disorder is described as: «individuals who have been subjected to intense coercive persuasions (for example: brainwashing, re-education, indoctrination during periods of imprisonment, torture, long political detentions, involvement in sects/cults or terrorist organizations) can demonstrate prolonged modifications of, or conscious questions regarding, one's own identity". Philippe Parquet (Perrotta 2016, p. 116), has elaborated, in this regard, a specific grid of criteria, within which at least five out of nine must be met in order to affirm that there is an ongoing mental conditioning:

1. break with the modalities of the previous behaviors, of conduct and judgment, with values, individual, family and collective social relationships;

2. cessation of any relationship with the previous life and acceptance by the individual that his personality, his emotional, cognitive, rational, moral and social life are shaped by suggestions, injunctions, orders, ideas, concepts, values and doctrines imposed by a third party or institution;

3. adhesion and unconditional affective, behavioral, intellectual, moral and social loyalty to a person, group or institution;

4. complete, progressive and total availability of one's life to a person, group or institution;

5. increased sensitivity over time to the ideas, concepts, prescriptions, injunctions and orders of a doctrine, and possibly the use of these in proselytizing practices;

6. expropriation of the abilities of a person with affective anesthesia, alteration of judgment, loss of references, values and critical spirit;

7. alteration of freedom of choice;

8. impermeability to opinions, attitudes, values of the external

environment with the impossibility of calling into question and promoting change;

9. inducement to carry out acts which are seriously prejudicial to the person, acts which previously were not part of the subject's life. These acts are no longer perceived as harmful or in contrast with the values and customs generally accepted by society. Sometimes participation in a sect results in psychiatric disorder, other times psychological support is needed. We have seen what are the social and psychological factors that push a person to take an interest in sects and new religious groups. Not all groups of Satanists can be called sects, because sects[33]have specific characteristics. They are characterized primarily by this process of mental manipulation, by its rigid and pyramidal structure, by the presence of a leader and by closure towards the outside world. Some groups of Satanists remain simple groups of people united by the same unease and desires, and sometimes small groups are far more dangerous than the big organized sects.

CHAPTER THREE

CRIMINAL SATANISM

"Evil has no substance of its own, but is only the defect, excess, perversion, or corruption of that which has substance." (John Henry Newman)

The Italian Constitution, among the fundamental principles, protects freedom of religion. Each person is free to choose which religion to profess, as long as he does not engage in behavior that can harm others. In fact, in article 8 of the Italian Constitution we read:

"All religious denominations are equally free before the law. Religious denominations other than Catholic have the right to organize themselves according to their own statutes, insofar as they do not conflict with the Italian legal system. Their relations with the state are regulated by law on the basis of agreements with the relative representations."

Again, in article 19:

"Everyone has the right to freely profess their religious faith in any form, individual or associated, to propagate it and to practice

worship in public or private, provided that these are not rituals contrary to morality."

What does "morality" mean? We can define it as the most common and most widespread way of behaving within a given society and in a given historical period, which is consistent with the ethical-moral complex. To give a content to this concept, then, it is necessary to refer to the social context existing in a certain historical period and to the ethical-moral principles and values of that community. For this reason, the majority orientation of the jurisprudence thinks that it is not possible to give the word "morality" a unique, eternal and immutable content, since it can be filled with correct contents only by referring to the historical, social and moral contingency of a community. In the Italian Constitution the term «morality» is mentioned twice: in article 19 and article 21 · [34] In these cases, the limit is placed in relation to decency and the violation of sexual modesty[35]. Finally, article 20 establishes that the state cannot impose any type of legislative limitation on associations which profess a particular cult:

"The ecclesiastical character and purpose of religion or worship of an association or institution cannot be the cause of special legislative limitations, nor of special tax liens for its constitution, legal capacity and any form of activity."

Therefore, we can affirm that religious sects, including satanic ones, are not prohibited by our system, which protects freedom of worship, but to be prohibited is the possibility that these groups, in an attempt to pursue their religious belief, implement behaviors that violate our penal code and morality, which is made to coincide, in this case, with sexual modesty. In particular, article 19 states that "rites" contrary to morality are prohibited, therefore religious sects are considered free to preach and propagate any idea, even contrary to morality, but not to celebrate rites and perform acts that the violate the law. The violation, therefore, is linked to the ritual/behavioral and non-ideological sphere. The massive growth of small groups or real religious organizations in recent decades has pushed the European Parliament to deal with sects and new religions. On February 5, 1992, Recommendation 1178 "on sects and new religious movements"[36] was approved, as concern about the activities of some religious groups, which disturb public order, increased. Governments wondered if legislation was needed to circumscribe and limit the freedom of sects. The path that led to the Recommendation took place in several stages:

• the Assembly was alerted by various associations and families who were committed to defending the victims of the activities of sects;

• accepted the invitation to the Council of Europe by the European Parliament in the Cottrell report to consider this problem;

• asked all member states to indicate which practices they follow and what the problems are;

• considered that the freedom of conscience and religion protected by article 9 of the European Convention on Human Rights made specific legislation on sects inapplicable, because it would interfere with this fundamental right;

• considered that a valid response to the problems encountered was the adoption of specific educational and legislative measures;

• recommended that the Committee of Ministers invite all member states to adopt various measures, including: an education program that includes information on all major religions and their main variants, on personal and social rights to be respected at all times and establishment of independent organizations to collect and disseminate information on sects and new religious movements.

Seven years after Recommendation 1178, in 1999, the European Parliament[37]had to go back to the topic again, because the number of people who joined religious groups was constantly increasing and the criminal reach of some of these groups was no longer a probability, but a certainty. Here, with the Council of Europe report on sects (1999), member states are requested:

1) the establishment of information centers on groups of a religious, esoteric or spiritual nature;

2) to include, in school curricula, information on the history and philosophy of important schools of thought and of religion in general;

3) the use of normal criminal and civil law procedures against illegal practices carried out in the name of groups of a religious,

esoteric or spiritual nature;

4) to encourage the establishment of non-governmental organizations for the victims, or families of the victims, of these groups;

5) to take firm positions against any discriminatory action or thought towards minorities and at the same time to encourage a spirit of tolerance and understanding towards all religious groups.

The Assembly also requested that a European Observatory be set up on groups of a religious, esoteric and spiritual nature, which would facilitate the collection and exchange of information between national observers and provide useful information to all citizens to avoid falling into seven o'clock trap. In Italy a voluminous report entitled "Seven religious and new magical movements in Italy" was published in 1998, after two years of investigation by the Department of Public Security, presented by the Minister of the Interior Giorgio Napolitano to the Commission for Constitutional affairs in the Chamber of Deputies. The relationship is divided into two parts. The first part describes the sectarian phenomenon and related social concerns, possible dangers and criminal connections, information on terminology, types of main sects and number of affiliates. In the second part, however, all 76 new religious movements and 61 new magical movements that have been detected are described. According to the speakers, the most worrying groups are the psycho-sects, since they would be able to provoke a complete mental manipulation of the adepts, which would lead them to madness and economic ruin. In fact, these groups are accused of wrongfully enriching themselves to the detriment of affiliates, blinded by the brainwashing they are subjected to.

The relation was drawn up with several purposes. In addition to the preventive one, it was necessary to study the activity of these groups considering the imminent year 2000, in which the Church celebrated the jubilee and the end of the millennium. The Ministry of Interior was concerned about public order and national security problems. Terrorist episodes or manifestations of religious fanaticism were not unlikely.

1. Satan in the criminal law

"What is it in absinthe that makes it a separate cult? The effects of its abuse are totally distinct from those of other stimulants. Even in ruin and in degradation it remains a thing apart: its victims wear a ghastly aureole all their own, and in their peculiar hell yet gloat with a sinister perversion of pride that they are not as other men."
(Aleister Crowley)

The Italian criminal law does not exactly include a satanic crime, as happens with other European laws. In England, for example, there is the cult crime model, a "ritual crime", whereby crimes committed by reason of adherence to some form of worship are treated and punished like all other crimes. In Italy a similar case does not exist, but we know that the Satanist religion implies a series of actions and behaviors that can certainly take the form of various types of crime, some of which are of serious criminal relevance. Today as today it would be unrealistic to think that there are no satanic groups, just as it is to think that there are as many as were registered in 1998 by the Department of Public Security, or as many as were detected by the Report on Satanism in Italy of the Telefono Antiplagio (Telephone Anti-plagiarism) (2004)[38]. Telefono Antiplagio has drawn up a report starting from the reporting calls received in ten years of activity. At the end of this report, it criticized the work done by the Ministry of the Interior, which would have identified a dozen satanic-luciferian groups in Italy, for a total of 200 followers, and speculates that instead there is a number of 2000 or 3000 followers. Although it is true that the search by the Ministry of the Interior may not have been able to intercept all the religious groups and their members, leaving out an important dark number[39] of followers and crimes, it is equally true that the number resulting from the Report, based only on the phone calls receipts, of which 95% anonymous (therefore unverifiable and hypothetically repeatable) is similarly far from reality. Above all, we cannot think that a social phenomenon remains unchanged over the years. Satanism had its maximum expansion in the 80s and 90s of the last century until the year 2000, then slowly decayed. This happened because many satanic groups were linked to the belief of the imminent return of the Antichrist, which would have manifested itself with the arrival of the new millennium. Today it is reasonable to think that the numbers of followers of satanic sects are no longer so numerous, but we certainly cannot say that the phenomenon has died out. Barresi (2004, pp. 188-192) made an analysis of all the criminal offenses of which the devil's followers could be guilty in carrying out their ritualistic practices:

1. Article 403 "Offenses against a religious confession through the vilification of people" (fine from € 1,000 to € 5,000): protects those who profess any religious profession from the offenses and insults of the Satanists;

2. Article 404 "Offenses against a religious confession by violating or damaging things" (fine from 1,000 to 5,000 euros): when churches, other religious sites and objects of any religious confession are ruined and defaced;

3. Article 405 "Disruption of religious functions of the cult of a religious confession" (up to 2 years): in the event that the Satanists want to disturb some religious function, ceremony or practice;

4. Article 407 "Violation of a sepulcher" (up to 5 years): Satanists, especially necrophiles and necrophages, incur this crime when they intend to obtain the corpses necessary for the rituals;

5. Article 408 "Violation of tombs" (up to 3 years): this crime is incurred when graves are looted or cemeteries are profaned as sacred places;

6. Article 410 "Violation of a cadaver" (up to 6 years): if a corpse is defaced or mutilated;

7. Articles 411 "Destruction, suppression or removal of a corpse" (up to 7 years), 412 "Concealment of a corpse" (up to 3 years), 413 "Illegitimate use of a corpse" (up to 6 months): all these crimes they can be performed if a body is taken for their rituals;

8. Article 416 "Criminal association" (up to 15 years): three or more Satanists who meet and associate in order to commit crimes can incur this crime;

9. article 527 "Obscene acts" (from 5.000 to 30.000 euro): if the members decide to make public orgies;

10. Article 564 "Incest" (up to 8 years): all members of a satanic sect who carnally join their offspring risk this penalty;

11. Article 566 "Supposition or suppression of state" (up to 10 years): all parents who decide not to report their offspring to the registry office are at risk of this penalty, in order to use them as they wish during their hidden career ;

12. Article 572 "Ill-treatment in the family or towards children" (up to 6 years): this is perhaps the most immediate consequence after parents decide to introduce their children to the sect;

13. Article 575 "Murder" (minimum 21 years): ritual murder is rare but not non-existent;

14. Article 578 "Infanticide in conditions of material and moral abandonment" (from 4 to 12 years): if a Satanist sacrificed his own child immediately after childbirth;

15. Article 579 "Murder of the consenter" (from 6 to 15 years): it

could happen that, through mechanisms of mental manipulation, one or more members are convinced that their death could lead them to safety;

16. article 580 "Instigation or aid to suicide" (from 5 to 12 years): as above, when adepts are made to believe that their suicide can free them;

17. Article 609 bis "Sexual violence" (5 to 10 years): this includes cases in which the Satanist, more often the priest, rapes the victim during the ritual of the Black Mass;

18. Article 609c "Sexual acts with minors" (from 5 to 10 years): as above, but referred to harm to minors;

19. Article 609d "Corruption of minors" (up to 5 years of age): concerns those who perform sexual acts in front of minors;

20. Article 609g "Group sexual violence" (from 6 to 12 years): involves those Satanists who engage in group rape during a black Mass, to the detriment of a single victim;

21. article 610 "Private violence" (up to 4 years): followers who, with violence or threat, force someone to act against their will;

22. Article 613 "State of incapacity procured by violence" (up to 1 year): this is the case in which a person is induced into a state of incapacity to understand or want by hypnotic suggestion or the use of alcohol and drugs;

23. article 624 "Theft" (up to 3 years): Satanists often carry out thefts inside churches, to obtain hosts, chalices and sacred

vestments to be profaned during the rites of the Black Masses;

24. Article 638 "Killing or damaging of other people's animals" (up to 1 year): it often happens that animals are sacrificed during the rites;

25. Article 639 "Defacing and soiling of other people's things" (up to 1 year): adepts who divulge their beliefs on the walls of buildings, religious and otherwise, incur this crime;

26. Article 643 "Circumvention of incapacitated people" (from 2 to 6 years): mechanisms of mental manipulation are more effective on already weak people, so groups of Satanists prefer to lure minors and mentally disabled people;

27. Article 661 "Abuse of popular credulity" (from € 5,000 to € 15,000): it is the crime committed by magicians and sorcerers who disclose their beliefs, their magical abilities or intermediary positions with evil demons for profit.

28. article 724 "Blasphemy and outrageous demonstrations towards the dead" (from € 51 to € 309): the blasphemy today is punished against any divinity, not only that of the Catholic creed. As with the first crimes on this list, however, it is rare for the Satanist to blaspheme against a divinity other than the Catholic one;

29. article 728 "Treatment suitable to suppress the conscience or the will of others" (arrest up to 6 months): in this type of crime the activities of those Satanists aimed at reducing other members of the

group into a state of hypnosis or narcosis, to then use it during the rites. Unlike art. 613, in this case, the victim is willing.

Criminologically speaking, what must frighten the police offices, rather than all these types of crimes, even quite serious ones, is what precedes them. The one who chooses Satanism is a person who tends to have relational problems with the outside world, who needs to express himself in a dimension in which he is free to vent his fantasies and enlarge his already damaged ego. They will commit acts of violence towards themselves, self-harming, or towards others, giving vent to their anger and their need for power, prevaricating and damaging the other. As more problematic personalities meet and form a group, the group becomes the dimension in which they can justify all their perversions and fantasies. When all the members of the group share the difficulty in relating to the outside world, the group will be the dimension in which to mirror themselves, it will give them a personality in which to recognize themselves and the strength to undertake and persevere in deviant or criminal conduct.

2. Sexual perversions and satanic crimes

"Bunch together a group of people deliberately chosen for strong religious feelings, and you have a practical guarantee of dark morbidities expressed in crime, perversion, and insanity."

(H. P. Lovecraft)

"Satanists present perversion in certain areas of the personality, including those related to pleasure and pain. Perversions have an important criminogenic significance, because they push, and sometimes justify, the perpetrator of the crime. Perversion can be defined as a "deviation from the *normal* sexual act, understood as coitus aimed at achieving orgasm through genital penetration with a person of the opposite sex" (Laplanche Pontalis, in Cantelmi Cacace 2007). Starting from this definition, it is reasonable to think that the definition of "normal" is strictly linked to the historical and social context in which we live. Think of homosexuality: in the past, it was considered a sexual perversion, but today this vision of homosexuality has been overcome. According to the Diagnostic and Statistical Manual of Mental Disorders (DSM), sexual perversions, called paraphilias, are all those sexual practices that are preferred and replaced by the copula and represent the only way for the person to experience sexual pleasure. A paraphilic person takes sexual pleasure only if he carries out his perversion.

"It is only by way of pain one arrives at pleasure." (Marquis de Sade)

Let's now see some of the sexual perversions that occur most often within satanic sects and which lead, for obvious reasons, to the execution of crimes, murders of a sexual nature and unusual practices during the Black Masses:

• anthropophagy: eating human flesh when the victim is still alive;

• exhibitionism: the person takes pleasure in showing his genitals, or takes pleasure in being looked at during a sexual act. Satanists, especially recreational/sexual ones, take pleasure in showing and looking at each other during ritual orgies;

• fetishism: sexual pleasure is connected not to the living person in its entirety but to a single part of the body or an external object. In the most pathological cases, the person cannot reach orgasm except in the presence of the fetish;

• satyriasis and nymphomania: the first refers to the man, the second to the woman. It is an abnormal sexual drive, an uncontrolled desire for sexual activity. Given the orgiastic practices of satanic sects, it is not uncommon for people with this disorder to choose to join a sect to vent their libido, feeling legitimized;

• voyeurism: pleasure derives from watching a sexual act. Again, people with this disorder may join a satanic sect to assist and watch during orgiastic moments;

• masochism: sexual pleasure is linked to the physical or moral pain of the subject, who feels pleasure in being beaten, submissive or humiliated. Among the many masochistic practices there are some that more than others are used by Satanists, such as urophagy (drinking urine), coprophagia (eating feces) or dermatophagia (eating dirty nails, skin of hands and feet). The sense in which Satanists enjoy these practices is to want to outrage, overthrow, desecrate and subvert normal social customs;

• sadism: sexual pleasure is given by causing suffering and pain to the other;

• necrophagy: eating corpses meat, practiced during some black Masses because it is believed that, after the ritual murder, engulfing the sacrificed corpse brings the adept closer to the malignant powers and increases its magical power;

• necrophilia: sexual arousal is linked to the moment in which one joins carnally with a corpse. This practice is even more widespread than necrophagy since sexual practices are of considerable importance in satanic rites and, if you think about it, joining with a corpse is the most aberrant thing you can think of, absolutely against nature and against the Church;

• necromania: morbid attraction towards death, corpses and everything that concerns them. It is a very dangerous perversion, which also involves the whole Satanist world, morbidly attracted to all that is dark and unhealthy;

• necrosadism: sexual perversion in which pleasure is linked to committing sadistic and violent acts on human and animal corpses. During some black Masses, dissecting a corpse is a propitiatory act;

• pedophilia: sexual attraction for children and young people, of both sexes;

• pedonecrophilia: form of necrophilia for which the subject feels pleasure only in the rape of corpses of children, and not of adult corpses;

• pica: a psychological disorder characterized by an appetite for substances that are largely non-nutritive, such as ice (pagophagia); hair (trichophagia); paper (xylophagia) drywall or paint; sharp objects (acuphagia); metal (metallophagia); stones (lithophagia) or soil (geophagia); glass (hyalophagia); feces (coprophagia) and chalk; in our case, it consists in eating parts of the human body or its products, such as skin, blood, sweat, urine, feces, earwax, saliva, pus. For Satanists, body fluids are of great importance, as well as why taking them is contrary to normal social customs, because they are thought to have precise magical powers;

• vampirism: sadistic sexual perversion, with decidedly psychopathic traits, which leads a subject to kill people to suck their blood.

2.1 Pedophilia and Satanism

"Physical experiences, lacking the joys of love, depend on twists and perversions of pleasure. Abnormal pleasures kill the taste for normal ones." (Anais Nin)

Often we hear about child abuse during black masses, and often satanic sects are linked to pedophilia, rape and the sacrifice of children. In concrete terms, a link exists. The child is a being with a pure, uncontaminated and innocent soul. For Satanists, sex is the most effective way of approaching evil spirits. Penetrating a child, uncontaminated and pure, is the practice that most gratifies Satan. In this sense, it would not be correct to speak of pedophilia, since it is a very specific sexual disorder, in which the subject experiences sexual excitement by thinking or acting of sex on children and children of pre-pubescent age. Satanists abuse children for specific sacrificial and propitiatory purposes and, unlike pedophiles, it is not certain that they suffer from this sexuality disorder. In fact, ritual sexual abuse is not linked to sexual gratification, as the purpose of the act, but to the sacrifice of the child to the devil. Furthermore, children are chosen because they are more easily manipulated. What differentiates ritual sexual abuse from simple abuse are the manipulation and conditioning techniques adopted and the victim's initiation into Satanism. Children are often sons and daughters of Satanists who are already members of the sect, they are from zero to six years old, and suffer repeated violence from many subjects, both men and women. The victim's manipulation mechanism starts from a very young age, and lasts several years since the sect manages to maintain control over the child in different ways, through affection, punishment, silence, blackmail, embarrassment, threats, violence. Right from the start, the child is accustomed to frequent enemas and washes to relax the muscles, and then moved away from the mother, so that the attachment bond is broken and the baby begins to become attached to the various members of the sect, which are internalized as positive figures of reference. When the child is four years old, he begins to attend black mass rituals. During the first part, when the devil's invocation formulas are recited, he is passed into the hands of the adepts, arranged in a circle. At the end of the ritual he is then forced to watch the sexual practices of the adult members, and then immediately sent to sleep. Thus, the first form of psychological abuse begins: the child is confused and terrified by what he has seen, he cannot give an explanation, and at the same time this becomes normal for him, because he is forced to regularly attend these ceremonies. The purpose of this first psychological abuse is to subdue and condition him to the point that he can no longer resist. When the child is ready, he begins to take an active part in the ritual, being penetrated and abused in turn by the priest and other members of the cult, both men and women. Ritual sexual abuse becomes methodical, and psychological abuse continues. The goal of the sect, in order to initiate the child into Satanism, is to take possession of his individuality and shape it at will. The child will grow up with a distorted world view. Natural references, the natural attachment process and normal growth processes are completely distorted. The family is not perceived as it should, since incestuous sexual intercourse takes place within it, and the child himself is abused by his parents. The cartoon characters and those of fantasy, which children like so much, are misrepresented. The abusers disguise themselves as Bugs Bunny, Santa Claus or Mickey Mouse while practicing violence on the victim, who negatively internalizes characters normally seen as good-natured and automatically projects a feeling of terror and dismay towards the external society, increasingly depending on the coven.

3. The clues to look for

"You're a tourist in sexual perversion. I'm a prisoner there."
(Louis C. K.)

In Italy there are a series of unsolved cases of satanic matrix, which are not resolved because it is not possible to give the correct interpretation of the crime scene and the clues. On the other hand, however, there is a long series of crime scenes that have been found rich in satanic symbols, without the authors being followers of the cult of Satan, with the simple intent to confuse the investigations. For these reasons, knowing that Satanist culture has a centuries-long history, knowing how varied it is and how many interpretative strands have arisen over the centuries, it is essential that the investigative activity is carried out with the help of an expert. It happens to be faced with crime scenes with symbols and objects related to satanic symbolism (inverted crosses, pentacles, images of Baphomet, number 666), episodes that have been guided by bizarre and cruelty (mutilations, defacements, ingestion and use blood, urine, and stools) or where it is evident that orgies and other sexual acts have occurred. It is not said, however, even in such circumstances, that the perpetrators of the crime are members of a satanic sect.

3.1 Satanic calendar, moon phases and days of the week

"Madness doesn't get off wearing gloves. It needs to feel skin on skin, smell the blood and shit as it brings itself off." (Benjamin R. Smith, Atlas)

To understand if you are faced with a crime of satanic matrix or not, the first thing to do is to compare the date of the crime with the occultist calendar (Cantelmi Cacace 2007, p. 69):

- October 31st. It is considered the "New Year of Satan", according to an ancient popular belief the souls of the dead return to visit their homes, so it is possible to have a contact with them. It is the right night to ask the Devil for advice, approval and protection. It is the most important event of the year, in which Beelzebub will fulfill all their wishes.

- December 13. It is the shortest day of the year.

- December 21. It is the winter solstice, and according to the pagan tradition the spirits of air and water are released everywhere.

- February 2. It is the "Night of Candlemas", also called "Festival of Lights", in which candles and other objects are consecrated; this objects will be used for rituals until the following year; also, the new followers are initiated into the sects.

- March 21. It's the spring equinox.

- April 30. It is the *Walpurgis Night*, which marks the beginning of the esoteric summer. A Mass is dedicated to propitiatory rites, to success, to the accumulation of goods, money and wealth. On this night all the spirits of Evil are invoked, and revenge is celebrated on the Law of Good, whereby white magic has no power on this date, which is controlled exclusively by the evil powers.

- June 24. Rites are held throughout the night that protect adepts and curse enemies.

- June 25. It is considered the night of magic.

- July 31. It is the date on which the longest and most important Sabbath is practiced, dedicated to the removal of external evil influences.

- August 1. It is the day when, according to tradition, Lucifer was precipitated from heaven to the underworld.

- 23 or 29 September. It should coincide with the autumn equinox. It is the night in which demonic knowledge is celebrated.

Still regarding the calendar, each magic ritual requires strict observance of the moon phases and the days of the week, since each has its own meaning. At each cycle, the moon goes through 4 phases and the total duration of the cycle is 29, 5 days.

The moon phases are four:

a) New Moon: suitable for spells related to blessings, to start something new;

b) Crescent Moon: it is the transition from the new moon to the full moon and is suitable for growth and novelty, therefore ideal for spells aimed at creating and producing;

c) Full Moon: ideal for spells related to positive feelings, knowledge, protection and prosperity;

d) Waning moon: ideal for finalizing spells which have as their object the removal of an obstacle, the elimination or release from someone or something. The waning moon is the most appropriate for black magic spells.

As for the days of the week:

a) Monday, the day of the Moon, suitable for spells related to travel, changes, strengthening sentimental relationships and finding a reconciliation;

b) Tuesday, Mars day, suitable for spells related to quarrelsome and war, quarrels, pain and suffering, disharmonies, contrast and destruction;

c) Wednesday, Mercury's day, suitable for spells related to the protection of one's property and business, the arts, science and positive energies related to knowledge;

d) Thursday, Jupiter's day, suitable for spells related to satisfactions, prizes, awards, friendship and health;

e) Friday, Venus day, suitable for spells related to loving, affective and social feelings;

f) Saturday, the day of Saturn, suitable for spells related to destruction, abandonment, hatred, disasters and death, possessions and visions;

g) Sunday, the day of the Sun, suitable for spells related to success and money, to victory over enemies and hostilities, finding the necessary forces to overcome obstacles.

It is very likely that the Satanists choose Tuesday or Saturday to celebrate their rituals and perform any criminal actions. The hours of the day and night also have a specific meaning. To celebrate the Black Masses, night hours are preferable.

3.2 Other clues

"Perversion is the erotic form of hatred." (Diane Ackerman)

To make sure we are faced with a satanic crime scene and not a simply bizarre, sadistic or perverse crime scene, we report a part of the card prepared by Dale Griffis for the American police (Mastronardi et al 2006, p. 71) :

Indications that can be found on the scene in the case of black occult practices in general:

1. Signs of desecration of Christian symbols (like inverted crosses);

2. Signs of ritual use of stolen Christian sacred objects, which are treated blasphemously;

3. Use of candles;

4. Satanic drawings and engravings on the ground and on the walls;

5. Writings in unrecognizable alphabets;

6. Mutilation of animals, including the removal of parts of the body such as the heart, tongue, ears;

7. Signs of use of animal parts (feathers, hairs, bones) to form marks on the ground;

8. Absence of blood on the ground where a killed animal is found, or on the carcass of the sacrificial animal;

9. Altar with typical satanic cult objects (candles, chalices, knives);

10. Mutilated voodoo dolls, sometimes with pins attached;

11. Cups or mugs, filled with powder or colored liquids;

12. Human skulls, with or without fixed candles;

13. Occult ceremony clothes, especially if intensely colored in black, white, scarlet;

14. Rooms decorated in black and red;

15. Books on Satanism, on the magic ritual.

In the case of investigations into a murder, these clues may be significant:

1. Location and position of the corpse;

2. Lack of parts of the body;

3. Location of wounds and cuts on the corpse;

4. Burns or burn scars;

5. Drops of wax on the victim or on the ground;

6. Oil, incense or perfumes found on the corpse;

7. Animal or human residues found on the victim;

8. Blood (drops, quantities);

9. Contents of the victim's stomach (analysis of the absorbed substances).

Griffis also suggests how to go about investigating a ritual crime scene:

Outdoor scene:

1. The outer perimeter is sometimes marked with white, red and black strings;

2. Symbols drawn on trees, walls, etc. .; it is necessary to detect their color;

3. Detect any body dyes, smoke bombs, blank bombs;

4. Look for a circle of nine feet (or three meters) in diameter within which there may be a pentagram or a second circle eight feet (or two and a half meters) in diameter. The dimensions of the figures will be reduced if space is scarce. If there is a staff, the observation point will be the southern tip. The altar will be at the western point of the circle. If there is a ring that bears traces of fire, it will be useful to dig under it for three feet, because something has probably been buried there;

5. Check if there is a path leading from the circle to a source of water;

6. Look for any stakes used to tie the victim to the ground with the head facing the water and with open arms. Look for animal cages and forks from which animals can hang;

7. Be careful not to enter the consecrated perimeter ritually unless you are sure that there are no pitfalls.

Indoor scene:

In addition to carrying out the same investigations as outside, check if there are refrigerators with containers that contain, or may have contained blood. Check for hypodermic needles, any parts of a human or animal body. Any particular extravagance or oddity can constitute an indication of Satanism, when it corresponds in some way to the ideology of Satanism itself.

3.3 Ritual murder

"Unanimous hatred is the greatest medicine for a human community." (Aeschylus, Eumenides)

We know that, of all the deviant and criminal activities carried out by sects, murder is at the bottom of the list. It is very likely that individuals who end up deciding to join a group of Satanists have sexual perversions. But individual atypical paraphilias, however, are unable to degenerate the usual religious practices into ritual murders only by themselves. What is a ritual murder? It is "a murder committed by a subject who kills one or more people, called sacrificial victims, to offer them as a sacrifice to a supernatural entity in exchange for spiritual benefits or earthly products" (Barresi 2006, p. 207). It is of fundamental importance to ask the malefic divinity par excellence for favors, profits and advantages. Sometimes it is enough to sacrifice an animal, other times the victim must be a person. The requests made during the sacrifice hardly ever show up in reality. In this way the Satanists, frustrated, will be forced to enter a vicious circle for which they will repeat the sacrificial murders in a serial way, because they believe that the last sacrifice did not satisfy the devil. If it is true that some paraphilia does not bring a coven to perform ritual murders, it is equally true that all ritual murders of a sexual nature are moved by paraphilias. The risk of a simple group of Satanists becoming a group of serial killers increases if the members are all affected by the same sexual perversion. Of all the above, the most dangerous is surely necromania. The necromaniac takes pleasure in causing someone else's death. While the sadist feels pleasure only in seeing the victim suffer, which however remains alive, the necromaniac experiences orgasm at the sight of the blood and death of his victim. In fact, there have never been any crime scenes from ritual murders where the victim was killed with a gun. Assassins must take pleasure in causing the death of others, and for this reason they prefer to use their hands or weapons, especially knives. However, to continue to delineate the criminological profile of satanic crimes, Barresi (ibid), has listed five guiding reasons to better understand the personality of the murderer who commits a satanic serial ritual murder:

1. schizophrenic motivation (MTS), in which psychotic and

paranoid subjects live dissociative states and perpetual escape from reality, for which they commit murders also following sensory illusions;

2. religious motivation (MR), in which the subject is so much subjugated by his own immense faith and subjected to the divinity that he undertakes, without asking questions, any mystical mission. This motivation can be of two types:

a) self-induced: the subject decides for himself his mission and mystical path;

b) hetero-induced: the subject receives from his boss the mission to be accomplished, which can often lead to ritual murder. In this case we speak of "serial ritual murder by induction";

3. paraphilic-sexual motivation (MPS), in which the subject experiences sexual gratification in an atypical way, for which his sexual drive can push him to carry out "murders for libido" (or lust murder), and of which the sexual perversion more necromania is certainly dangerous;

4. ego-centric motivation (MEC), in which the subject is of the egotic-sadistic type, needs to feel superior, powerful, to subject and see someone else submissive and suffering. The perpetrator-victim relationship often culminates in a ritual murder;

5. symbolic motivation (MS), in which the subject feels he must kill members of a category deemed undeserving, such as priests or prostitutes, to take revenge or for greater ideological reasons.

Again, to continue with our criminological profile, Mastronardi (2006, p. 283) listed the possible types of ritual murder, linked to the reasons for which they are carried out:

• purifiers, negativities and sins of mankind;

• ingratiating the divinity, to achieve its sectarian goals;

• propitiator of control over life and death, performed for representative purposes for new adepts and to strengthen the self-esteem of those who perform it;

• orgiastic, at the beginning or end of the ritual orgies;

• thanking the divinity, after some request was made or granted;

• procurement of human material to be used for ritual purposes (tissues, biological liquids, bones, whole organs for ceremonies and potions, etc...).

Investigation is never a simple activity. In the specific case of ritual murder, in addition to following the standard procedures for all crime scene inspections, it is essential that those in charge does not leave out any clues, which assesses the exact location of all the elements that are part of the crime scene, without prejudice, and analyze them according to the most likely reconstruction. Too often the esoteric signs and symbols present at the scene of the crime are overlooked. With a careful analysis of the crime scene it is possible to interpret a symbology that can conduct investigations on a satanic track, even of a serial type. Most of all, in order to do this, due to the complexity and variety of the phenomenon, it is essential to invest in the training of law enforcement personnel, so that they can be able to recognize the hidden matrix of the murder and refer, in in this case, to expert investigators.

4. Conclusions

"I don't know what the heart is, not I: I only use the word to denote the mind's frailties." (Marquis de Sade)

In our study we have approached the dark world of Satanism and, in particular, of criminal Satanism. We can say that Satanism is a cult, a religion, characterized by a particular vision of the world antithetical to the Christian one and to common morality. Adopting the Satanist worldview and practicing this belief, however, does not necessarily mean committing a crime, because our Constitution protects freedom of worship and freedom of expression. It is illegal to condemn an ideology. There is a difference, then, between religious-style Satanism, typical of cult and esoteric rituals, and criminal-style Satanism, typical of those subjects who use satanic worship as a pretext to commit one or more crimes. In the first case, the choice of cult does not represent a criminal offense, unless rituals contrary to the law, public order or morality are carried out. In the second case, the offense is intrinsic in the activity carried out and is therefore prohibited by the Italian law. Satanism is often associated with the idea of "sects", but not all groups of Satanists can be labeled as such. We know that a sect, to be defined as such, must have very specific characteristics: proselytism, indoctrination of the new adept, love bombing, brainwashing and total enslavement of the adept to the leader and the entire sect. Not all satanic groups have these peculiarities and therefore it is not always correct to use the term satanic sects. However, this expression can be used in a broad sense, as was done in this study. An important element concerns the fact that, despite the media bombardment, aimed at attracting the interest of public opinion, morbidly attracted by the occult, horror and demonic, we have little news about the existence and presence, on our territory, of groups dedicated to satanic worship. The same goes for criminal groups: apart from a few very famous news events, official statistics do not reveal a large number of them. The episodes of satanic murders to which we can refer, we cannot define them as true satanic murders. The authors have always defined themselves as Satanists, without ever being so in substance. Satanism was an excuse to carry out a criminal conduct, also driven by psychic disorders and drug abuse. In fact, the homicidal dynamics show the absence of a real rituality, and a superficial knowledge of the Satanist culture. Maybe they were individuals who really believed in the devil, but they were certainly not Satanists in the strict sense of the term. Is it possible to prevent these crimes? Yes, if you listen to the uneasiness of today's youth, if you can offer them alternative ways of success to that of the satanic career, if you know the techniques of mental manipulation acted by sects, if you can interrupt them and, in general, if it is possible to intercept and monitor already formed and existing groups, before their activity precipitates the vortex of illegality.

CHAPTER FOUR

SATAN AND THE PERVERSE MIND:

Psychoanalytic considerations around satanic sects

Satanism and Perversion

"No one who, like me, conjures up the most evil of those half-tamed demons that inhabit the human breast, and seeks to wrestle with them, can expect to come through the struggle unscathed"
(Sigmund Freud, Dora: An Analysis of a Case of Hysteria)

Within the satanic sects, behaviors marked by violence, manipulation, pathological narcissism, paraphilias and antisociality can be found: these are also some of the predominant aspects of the "perverted" personality. Perversion is characterized by a certain destructiveness towards others and is carried out through malicious actions that can lead to crime. Evil would coincide with the achievement of "absolute power": it is no coincidence that the psychoanalyst Stoller (1978) defined perversion as "an erotic form of hatred or rather of hostility; that is, the desire to damage an object. The excitement comes from the awareness - conscious or unconscious - of the fact that someone is being hurt, that one needs to do harm, that one wants to do harm." Perversion is placed in a continuous and constant enigmaticity between deviation and subversion of the norm, between inability to conform and intentionality to want to move the limits consensually allowed, between disease and social phenomenon and of innovative customs, and finally between disjointed or contiguous conduct related to affective and erotic normality (Chasseguet-Smirgel, 1983). Perversion is to be understood, above all, on the relational level; in this regard, another psychoanalyst, Kernberg (1996), writes: "perversion is the recruitment of love in the service of aggression, the consequence of the predominance of hatred over love". In all cases of malignant perversion, as happens in some practices carried out in Satanism, the use of ritualized cruelty must be placed in the broader theme of human destructiveness, which is exercised more frequently against a weak and defenseless being and in erotic pleasure, which provides for a real dehumanization of the other. Malignant eroticism and destruction of the object are at the service of the death drive and the destructive component that exists in each person, but which in these subjects has triumphed over love for life and respect for others. In perversion there is therefore a real celebration of omnipotence ("I can do anything I want, even kill") and of the destructiveness that find shape in the negation of the other, or as De Masi says, in the "degradation of the object of love that transforms the person into a thing". In criminal conduct, in fact, the other does not exist as a person, but only as a target invested with a symbolic meaning, on which to move one's destructiveness. Blanchot (2003) writes: "All that perverse refers to others, he denies it. For example: pity, gratitude, love, all feelings that he destroys and, destroying them, he recovers all the force that he should have devoted to these impulses and, more importantly, derives from this work of destruction the principle of a real energy". What the pervert enjoys is not purely the pleasure that comes from sexuality, but the sexuality brought to that limit beyond which there is death. For Bataille, the perverted "entered the game that links eroticism to death". Therefore, the satisfaction of the pervert is obtained exclusively by the mistreatment and humiliation of the subject and can go as far as death. The eroticization of non-sexual activities represents the consequence of a deficit in the organization of the Self, a defect that the individual tries to compensate with fantasies or sexual behaviors aimed at preventing further psychic regression (Goldberg, 1998), even if the mechanism of sexualization has also been interpreted not as a defensive strategy, but as the expression of a deadly nucleus (De Masi, 1999), which seeks an "objectless" pleasure, therefore destructive, and which in this way generates the perverse character structure. As regards more directly the sexual perversions carried out in satanic cults and during rituals the following can be listed:

- anthropophagy: the eating of human flesh;

- necrophagy: the feeding of corpse meat, including that of the sacrificial victim, in order to increase magical power;

- necrophilia: having sex with corpses;

- necromania: morbid attraction for corpses;

- pedophile: to have relationships with corpses of children;

- necrosadism: sadistic acts on corpses;

- vampirism: sadistic perversion consisting in drinking a person's blood (killing him);

- picacism: in this case, it consists in eating parts or secretions of the human body. It is practiced in black masses, where the elixir is consumed, consisting of male and female sexual secretions

- sadism: feeling pleasure causing pain and pain;

- pedophilia: sexual attraction for children;

- masochism: sexual pleasure linked to the physical and moral pain experienced by the subject.

"Nothing holds love together like shared vice or collusive perversion" (Glen Duncan)

The perverse, like Satan, relates evil to pleasure; in this way, he "assures" a relationship of power towards the other, gains control of the other, can dominate his soul and his body. As Hirigoyen (2000) states, perverts make others suffer by "destroying" them, creating an atmosphere of unease and fear around them. In the perverse, the object relationship with the other is therefore missing, object relationship understood as the perception of the other as a person and other than himself. In particular, speaking of Satanism, we refer to people, groups or movements that in a more or less organized form practice the adoration and evocation of demons and/or of the Devil, meaning with the term "devil" the figure outlined in the framework of religions that adopt the Bible as the sacred text. If on the one hand, in groups that call themselves worshipers of Satan, there is a specific identity that adheres to the norms of the group, on the other hand, especially in satanic groups that commit heinous crimes such as sacrifices of people and / or murders, it lacks the whole feeling of responsibility: we are within a real context characterized by manipulation, abuse of the other and a lack of empathy, elements that can be identified in the perverse framework. One can also find, especially in the leaders of these sects, narcissistic needs of omnipotence, acts of extreme devotion in exchange for some particular salvation promised in the name of Satan or some other demon presented or even invented by him. For S. Freud (1919), the uncanny belongs to the sphere of anguish and terror. By behaving in this way, the perverse destroys the relationship with the other who is treated more as an object than as a person. Cruelty and a lack of guilt are further elements that describe the perverse personality: the other is used as an instrument of one's enjoyment, is "stripped" of its most human aspects and simply becomes an "instrument", a means by which to accomplish the own malicious actions. The pervert enjoys, in fact, the anguish of others: in this way, he can become the "master" of the other, or, enjoying the pain of another, he deludes himself into controlling him. From this description it is also observed how the element of antisociality is decisive within these sects, where real crimes can occur. In this regard, M. Strano (2003) distinguishes two types of crimes: on the one hand those committed by the leaders against the adepts who suffer them and on the other hand, the crimes committed by the adepts against other adepts or external persons to the sect. The first kind of crimes include:

- scams and fraud

- threats

- extortion

- kidnappings

- exploitation (of work and prostitution)

- injuries (caused during rituals)

- physical violence of various types

- drug dealing

- pedophilia

- sexual abuse

- induction to suicide

- murders

While the second type of crime includes:

- family crimes (e.g. lack of sustenance, abandonment, etc.)

- violence and injury to other followers during rituals

- possession and dealing of narcotic substances

- sexual abuse and pedophilia

- desecration of cemeteries

- mistreatment of animals

- thefts (e.g. hosts and other objects in churches)

- competition in scams and fraud

- information theft

- damage (churches and other premises)

"Every perversion has survived many tests of its capabilities."
(Louis C.K.)

John Milton, in the book "Paradise Lost" recalls how Satan was envious of God and how he had decided to become the usurper of heaven: in this passage, the author describes very well the implicit aspects of envy. The pervert, in fact, believes himself better than the others and has an altered vision of the world: the people around him become a source of narcissistic nourishment and must be exploited, manipulated, tortured and even killed. In this way, the perverse reinforces his pleasure of destruction by being free of moral scruples, of pity, of compassion and of remorse. We can find these elements right at the beginning of Milton's poem that begins with Satan's statement of his perverse program:

"If then his Providence

Out of our evil seek to bring forth good,

Our labor must be to pervert that end,

And out of good still to find means of evil"

In addition to the exploitation of the other, within these satanic sects, mental manipulation is also observed, that is, subjugating the other without scruples, often adopting techniques of mental conditioning and psychological suggestion, structuring pathological relationships characterized mainly by dynamics of destructive power aimed at the annulment of the victim's identity and its exploitation. In fact, in the dynamics of these groups, the individual will is canceled by the will of the group, especially if the sect is led by a leader who enjoys a certain affirmation. In general, however, as F. Barresi (2003) writes, "affiliates come together out of personal conviction and not so much due to external persuasive factors, except (...) the cases in which minors or people with psychic pathologies are involved to cloud their ability to understand and want or from personality profiles that make them particularly suggestible or manipulable". In particular, M. Strano (2003), recognizes some individual psychological variables of the adepts; they include:

- antagonism to the frustration of social inadequacy through belonging to a group (the sect) which deliberately generates in the followers the belief of being important, naturally only within the sect itself;

- charisma of leaders and complementary request for charismatic power by insecure subjects;

- reduction of anxiety through the acquired conviction of

otherworldly existences, immortality, etc.;

- increase in self-esteem following the learning of magical powers that allow a renewed ability to determine events and control the external environment;

- reduction of anxiety in situations of great psychological pain (following for example a family mourning);

- satisfaction of dependency and submission needs by subjects with particular personality profiles;

- opportunities for interpersonal relationships (also sexual) for subjects with particular relationship difficulties;

- loneliness and family breakdown;

- particular sensitivity to techniques of suggestion and operative conditioning (systematic reinforcement of useful behaviors by the charismatic leader).

"The desire to hurt the sexual object - or the opposite feeling, the desire is to hurt oneself - is a perversion of the most common sex life" (Sigmund Freud)

The Satanist, like the perverse, is also guided by division and separation: the term "devil", in fact, derives, through the Latin "diabolus", from the Greek "Διάβολος" which means "slanderer", but also "divide"; it was used in the Greek version of the Bible to translate the Hebrew ha-satan, "Satan", properly "adversary".

Lactantius writes: "Before creating the world, God conceived a spirit similar to him, full of the virtues of the Father. Then he conceived another in which the imprint of divine origin was canceled because he got stained with the poison of envy and therefore passed from Good to Evil (...). He was jealous of his older brother who, united with the Father, secured his affection. This being, who has become evil, is called Devil by the Greeks". Even in the perversion, for Freud, one can see the equivalents of a "satanic religion" or the "residues of an ancestral sexual cult". The same myth of Lucifer has often lent itself very well to symbolically exemplify the profound psychological situation that would characterize the perverse personality: he too rivals the Father-God, he wants to oust and dethrone him. The purpose of the perversion, in fact, as the psychoanalyst C. Smirgel (1984) reminds us, is to escape the human condition, trying to get rid of the paternal universe and the laws that follow from it: that is, the perverse tries to replace the creator father to wreak havoc and create a new universe where everything becomes possible. For the psychoanalytic interpretation of the Freudian school (Jones E., 1912; Rank O., 1914; Freud S., 1922) the Devil is considered as a representative of the father: the negative feelings of anger and hatred that the child experiences in towards the father, they are projected on an external figure, Satan, as well as the good and compassionate aspects of the father, form the image of God. Satan would be the result of the projections of the aggressive instincts of hatred and rancor that the child feels towards a limiting and frustrating father, or rather, a seductive and perverse father, cruel and liar, bearer of evil and mocking. For Jones E. (1912): "Belief in the Devil largely represents an externalization of two sets of removed desires (...): a: the desire to imitate some aspects of the father figure; b: the desire to challenge the father - in other words, emulation and hostility alternate" (Jones E., 1912, p. 145). Psychoanalysis has always taught that the relationship with the father is marked by ambivalence, by antagonistic forces: affection on the one hand and hostility and challenge on the other. This ambivalence also characterizes the relationship of the human being with the divinity: it is no coincidence that God and Satan were two originally identical figures and then split into two figures with opposite attributes (on the one hand the good, on the other the evil). The father, therefore, becomes the individual archetype of both God and the Devil. Even the very origins of Satanist theory were influenced by the widespread acceptance of dualism, that is, the belief that opposed beneficial divinities to malefic divinities, existing independently of each other. This division is characteristic of perversion, which is based on the division between good aspects of oneself, or in any case acceptable and accepted, and bad aspects. In fact, "the essence of the perverse impulse consists in transforming the good part into the bad part, preserving the appearance of goodness" (Meltzer, 1973). Furthermore: "the perverse impulse is linked to the criminal one through the desire to devalue and despise good objects" (Meltzer, 1973). Goldberg (1995) also considers perverse behaviors "on the one hand as useful for self-cohesion, on the other as a pathological condition that is expressed in the exploitation of others". The purpose of the pervert is therefore the destruction of reality and the ability to give and receive love. From a psychoanalytic perspective, the world of division and separation presupposes a three-dimensional psyche (Zipparri, 2000): between mother and son, the father-creator is introduced, a metaphor for incest. By rejecting the rules of reality and the adult world, the perverse refuses to submit to the "father" and the law he represents. The Devil also represents the container of drives removed and not accepted by consciousness. "(...). And certainly the devil is nothing but the personification of the unconscious drive life removed" (Freud S., 1908). "Spirits and demons (...) are only the projections of his emotions. He (the primitive man) transforms his affective positions into characters with which he populates the world, and then finds his own internal mental processes outside himself". Furthermore, for Freud, demons are nothing but "bad, repudiated desires, which derive from instinctual motions that have been pushed and removed." For C. G. Jung the Devil is the representative of the bad parts of man, psychologically corresponds to the Shadow (1948). Satan is the other side of the archetype of the Self, the other face of God. For CG Jung it is necessary to accept and face the Devil, just as in analysis it is necessary to accept and face the Shadow, if you want to continue along the difficult path to identification. The Devil therefore represents our psychic wounds and anxieties. The psychoanalyst Alfonso M. Di Nola (1980) adds that the demonic is the "dialectic between fullness of being and failure, between Eros and Thanatos, as moments of the enjoyment of existing and denying existence". Satan, like the perverse, is dominated by two internal ghosts: the animal and God. Like the animal, the perverse does not restrain instinct and is guided by an unlimited drive; just think of the orgies and sexual rites that are consumed within the Sabbaths and Black Masses. The goat is the animal considered par excellence "satanic"; in the Middle Ages the devil was represented with goat features: the devil was the fallen angel formed by the most terrifying features, out of contempt for God and his having created him in his time as an angel "in his image and likeness" (it seems that the identification of the devil with a goat is due to the Greek translation of the Bible, whereas a term meaning "wild goat, satyr, demon" was used to describe the devil's appearance).

"Where is the source of all money-sickness, and the origin of all sex-perversion? .... It lies in the heart of man, and not in the conditions." (D.H. Lawrence)

The perverse is dominated by chaos, a notion that has always opposed the biblical story of Genesis and perversion is understood here as rebellion against the divine norm; C.Smirgel (1987) writes: "the universe of perversion is opposed in every detail to that described in the text on which our Judeo-Christian civilization is based". Just think of the figure of the "Devil", who is intended as the one who gets in the way, who literally divides "who stands sideways" to the plan of God. In fact, the Devil starts the orgy and the guests mate, without distinction of sex and kinship. The pervert wants to impose a reality in which confusion and chaos prevail, and chaos becomes a metaphor for evil and the unknowable, or rather, the uncanny. The author underlines how perversions are a distortion of reality through the denial of differences between the sexes and between generations; that is, in the perversions all the differences cancel each other out, including those between what is good and what is bad. For Smirgel the world of the perverse is, therefore, a world that denies reality because it is a world without a father, in which the possibility of survival is delegated to the fantasy of fusion with the womb, in which everything is possible for the perverse, in an omnipotent existence in which the other disappears.

"I'm just like you

Made by him

Despised by they

I'm almost me

I'm nearly human

Pity me I'm almost a human being" Aurelio Voltaire - Almost Human)

CHAPTER FIVE

SATANISM BETWEEN CRIMINOLOGICAL EXEGIS AND NEWS

1. The Beasts of Satan

"Hell is empty and all the devils are here". (William Shakespeare, The Tempest)

Science defines "malleable" that material that can be permanently deformed without suffering structural changes or fractures. Isn't a young person, without form or substance, the equivalent of malleable matter in the reality of these days? Perfect in appearance, easily dismantled in being. Nowadays that of the sects is a phenomenon so widespread as to cause concern for many, including the Vatican, psychologists, psychiatrists and criminologists. But what is meant by sect? What are the mechanisms by which they act on people? How can a sect be defined from an anthropological and criminological point of view? Basically, there are some cardinal points around which a sect revolves: first of all, psychological coercion; in fact, more or less all types of sects exercise a strong psychological conditioning on members (or adepts) in order to make the latter docile up to passivity. The person who is part of a sect must not reason or have his own ideas but obey the teachings and the will of a "leader". Hence the second point: the existence of a charismatic leader, with great consideration of himself and with an ego out of the norm, which dictates the rules. Let us remember that sects are totalitarian and that their logic is very simple, that is, that the end always justifies the means. Finally, it is necessary to highlight that the wealth accumulated by the sect, by the members belonging to it, is never aimed at the benefits of the individual, but of the group. There are numerous studies that deal with the phenomenon of sects and, in some respects, not all agree. It is common opinion that the leader, the centerpiece of the sect, is almost always an enigmatic type with a strong and complex personality that has evolved from an often difficult and studded childhood. But not all scholars are of this opinion; for example, Anthony Storr argues that the leaders are solitary types and rejected by others, unable to make friends and endowed with a more developed egocentrism than normal people, even when they enter adulthood. All this causes numerous and pathological frustrations which are the vector of a natural excess of trust towards certain spiritual philosophies. In practice, the leader transforms insecurities into a spiritual experience that often results in disappointment and therefore pushes him to create his own, tailor-made spiritual philosophy in which he places himself at the center. This process is capable of transforming the insecure and good-for-nothing loner into a charismatic leader capable of conditioning other people. But what type of people are plagiarized from sects? The idea that the followers of a sect are individuals with a medium-low intellectual level is now obsolete and, indeed, some scholars have come to the conclusion that the affiliates of the sects are generally gifted with above-average intelligence. But then, for what reasons do these individuals submit themselves psychologically? Followers of sects often come from middle classes; they are extremely dissatisfied with the messages transmitted by traditional religions and they look for new cults, new emotions, new meanings and different spiritual visions. They need the charisma of a leader and they want to be guided to be aware of being part of something necessary and important: this combination often leads to absolute obedience. The illusions created by the gurus have no inhibitory brakes and, above all, they are not subject to criticism from the followers. The continuous search for spiritual newness does not necessarily lead to "false religions" but also to holistic philosophies, ufology, esotericism and much more so it becomes almost impossible to be able to catalog the various types of sects. The modus operandi with which the sects operate, regardless of the typology, remains always the same: the individual is immediately accepted into the group, making him feel an integral part of it so as to make the next step easier, that is to make him feel less and less master of his own life, his affections, possessions and, finally, his will. Once the metamorphosis is complete, the individual is ready to blindly believe the orders given by the leader of the sect, up to extreme gestures.

"*Monsters are real, and ghosts are real too. They live inside us, and sometimes, they win." (Stephen King)*

What do sociology and criminology say about it? Andrea Volpe was an eighteen year old like others who, five years later, became a murderer in the name of Satan. In the autumn of 2007 the Court of Cassation sentenced him to twenty years of imprisonment (sentence no. 45583 of 25 October). The same guilty sentence was pronounced against Pietro Guerrieri, also responsible, together with other defendants judged separately. Thanks to Volpe's testimonies during the trial, the authorities obtained important information on other crimes committed in the same period by the sect called *Beasts of Satan*. Volpe and Guerrieri were responsible for the murder of Fabio Tollis and Chiara Marino, who were members of Volpe's group; later it will be discovered that this cult practiced rites based on blasphemous sexual practices, with abuses of all kinds and the detriment not only of the non-followers, but also of those who were part of the sect. They were also convicted of illegal possession of cutting weapon and offending items, as well as illegal heroin detention. Journalists, following the start of the trial, wrote about "acid Satanism" as a typically youthful satanic cult for which, according to M. Introvigne, the devil is only an excuse to operate excesses and deprivations precisely through the abuse of drugs and alcohol. Volpe was also accused and convicted of the murder of Mariangela Pezzotta, his ex-girlfriend, killed with a .38 caliber gun on a new moon night. Law enforcement officials reported that the blow was so strong that it "completely erased her face." He was also responsible for the concealment of the corpse, illegal possession of common firearms and ammunition, home burglary, robbery, damage and incitement to suicide of Andrea Bontade, called "the traitor", who, after being drugged and humiliated for months by his companions, crashed at 180km/h against a wall (traces of braking on the asphalt will never be found, as proof of the fact that it was a likely voluntary gesture, certainly desperate). A confused picture, as a perfect mirror of the personalities of the subjects involved. In this messy affair, an ambiguous but perhaps not accidental constant cannot escape: the victims are all young people who knew and frequented Volpe. The bond as a precondition, affection as a starting point and hatred as the arrival point. Volpe, in his own words, was a "weak and violent person". On September 8, 2007, during an interview with the weekly "Gente" Volpe said: "*It would be easy to put all the blame on drugs, to say that we did what we did because we were unable to understand and want. After all, it would be a nice alibi to say «we killed because we were blown away and we no longer understood anything». But I believe that drugs have had only a minor influence on our actions. We were convinced of what we were doing. We were angry young people, with the desire to transgress and rebel against a society that had never committed itself to understanding each other*". Volpe alludes to a great truth: the boundary between the guilt of the person and that of society has become so blurred that it no longer allows us to understand so clearly who is ultimately to be put on the defendants' bench. And all those crazy and unjustifiable gestures made in the name of Satan can only be the result of a personal malaise that pushes those who live it to impose it on someone else. In a context of youthful deviance "it is not so impossible that we move from «playing» to being Satanists, to being aggressive, manipulative and finally getting carried away and playing God, arrogating the right to decide who lives and who dies" (quotidiano.net). Feeling masters of a choice, that of overwhelming the weakest to feel strong in a society that has looked at them as weak. And it doesn't matter, then, to call it Satanism or by any other name. How much Satan has to do with this whole story is the least important and most revelatory question at the same time. "Everything", we may answer. Instead, by studying the mechanisms behind the gestures of these deviant, repressed and drugged young people, the answer becomes "nothing". Satan is an expedient, a thin leaf that hides the malaise of those who kill in his name. There is only a group of young people, prey to personal tragedies, disappointments, existential doubts, failures in not being able to grasp what life, in a low voice, offered him. And here comes, as always and on tiptoe, the usual paradox of this life: the only true victims of Satan in this sad story are them. "Vile murder of defenseless victims" said the Cassation. However, overcoming the legal boundary, one cannot fail to grasp how no one was more defenseless than Andrea Volpe, a young boy devoured by fears and awareness, victim of a society that has never stopped making him fragile. Andrea Volpe, 11 years later, is converted to Christianity and prays to a God whose years before he had tried to steal the place.

2. The murder of Sister Laura

"I cannot follow you Christians; for you try to crawl through your life upon your knees, while I stride through mine on my feet."
(Charles Bradlaugh)

The recent Italian chronicles record another Satanist murder. On June 6, 2000, Milena De Giambattista, Veronica Pietrobelli and Ambra Gianasso, massacred "in the name of the devil" Sister Laura, 61, in the Park of the Giants' Pots, with 19 stab wounds. "I will ask God to forgive you..." were her last words. During the trial, the prosecutor arranged psychiatric reports, who considered all three affected by personality disorders, so as to make them unable to understand and want. The first instance sentence, issued on 9 August 2001, imposed eight and a half years for Veronica and Milena and the acquittal for Ambra, deemed incapable: in the second degree, the acquittal was reversed in sentencing at 12 years with an obligation to stay at a therapeutic community. Later the first criminal section of the Cassation made the sentence of 12 years and 4 months imprisonment definitive for Ambra, while eight and a half years in prison were sentenced for Milena and Veronica. On the evening of that June 2000, around 10 pm, Sister Laura left the convent to meet a girl who had told her that she needed her help following a violence she had suffered. It was a lie of Ambra

Gianasso, seventeen, to make the nun reach an isolated place where, together with her friends Veronica Pietrobelli and Milena De Giambattista, they would have given her in sacrifice to Satan. The young women initially hit her with a tile and ended up killing her with 19 stab wounds. It would be reasonable to believe that whoever wielded the weapon did not bother to kill, because killing was not the real purpose. Murder, however ambiguous and difficult to understand, is a means. Assassination is a tool to achieve the real goal: to give vent to anger, to the claim to prevail, to the desire to exaggerate. Death becomes a marginal concept that rests only in the corner of the story, for those who kill. The girls, not even adults at the time, all come from stories of disadvantaged families. They used to run away from their personal reality to get drunk, perform sacrilegious acts and listen to satanic rock. "I was disgusting" says Veronica in an interview with Panorama in April 2008. "I don't know why we did it. We wanted to overdo." At 16 she felt awkward and ugly, surrounded by many people but similar to none of them. "I wanted to let the world know that I was there because it didn't seem to notice." What appears different in this story is the denial by young women of belonging to a satanic sect. So Satan becomes only a symbol, as LaVey claimed, a pretext for exceeding. The girls did not care in the name of who to act, it only mattered to impose themselves, to feel strong.

3. The Children of Satan

"The one who runs from his shadows sleeps with the devil at night." (Robin Sacredfire)

Marco Dimitri is another name written in the history of those who acted in the name of the devil. Dimitri is the founder of the group "Children of Satan"; in January 1996 he was arrested, together with two other young men, on the charge of narcotizing and raping Elisabetta Dozza, ex-girlfriend of one of the accused, during a black mass. The boys were acquitted, but the court case had an important media reflection, and the news, as well as the city of Bologna, screamed ashamed. Dimitri was led to approach such a strange reality by his young and misunderstood personality. He himself declares, in an interview with the online newspaper Ristretti.org: "I was a restless teenager. I was orphaned at age 14. I was looking for answers in society but I could not find them and I was attracted by the beauty of the irrational, by the metaphysical. Hence the search for Satan, as a means of reaching and obtaining power. We were kids. We thought we would find the easy life through a sort of pact with the devil and then we played with it. "And that's exactly where the story changes. Dimitri's acquittal led to his immediate release after a brief stay in prison. The story, slowly, it was forgotten. There was no mention of Dimitri, nor of the Children of Satan. To date, anyone knows the story of the Beasts of Satan, but few seem to remember that of the Children. Everyone returned to their own life, Dimitri became a computer technician, and today he also lends his knowledge to private investigative agencies. A detail however distinguishes this protagonist from those of all the other events: many years have passed, Dimitri is no longer a boy with unconscious choices. Today he is 54 years old, he has a job and, potentially, all the maturity of any adult. In 2012 he even ran for political elections for Lazio with the list "Atheist Democracy". However, something else seems to suggest that very little has changed in the mind of this man, who continues to pursue his association under the name of Satan; he names the devil on numerous occasions, both in Italy and abroad, and organizes annual meetings with those who are part of his group. He is the only one, among those whose youth was spent in the name of Satan, to have found nothing intrinsically wrong with worshiping the devil. In his case, Satan's idolatry becomes a principle, not an expedient. What has Dimitri experienced that differentiates him from the others? The correct question would be, rather, what he did not experience. He did not experience the weight of the consequences of his actions, the condemnation and restriction of a value so longed for as freedom. He did not live that inner path that anyone found himself fighting, in the intimacy of thoughts and within the walls of a dark and small room. He did not experience that possibility of understanding and re-socializing. After all, in this case, no one can point the finger at poorly administered justice. However, one cannot avoid noting the diversity of his path and the reflection of this difference in his destiny compared to that of others. The truth is that Dimitri was never punished, because he did nothing wrong. The cult of Satan does not represent an offense, it is the Constitution itself that protects the freedom of worship. The paradox returns: the law protects the Satanist and condemns those who obstruct an ideology, even this one.

"Christianity may be good and Satanism evil. Under the Constitution, however, both are neutral. This is an important, but difficult, concept for many law enforcement officers to accept. They are paid to uphold the penal code, not the Ten Commandments... The fact is that far more crime and child abuse has been committed by zealots in the name of God, Jesus and Mohammed than has ever been committed in the name of Satan. Many people don't like that statement, but few can argue with it." *(Carl Sagan, The Demon-Haunted World: Science as a Candle in the Dark)*

Today Andrea Volpe says he is converted to Christianity; during his time in prison, he was able to study and obtain a degree, and thanks to his repentance the testimonies led to numerous discoveries in the investigations against the Beasts of Satan. The same goes for Ambra, who obtained a degree after finishing the five-year high school course. Young people who paid dearly for their crazy gestures, who lost the freedom and light-heartedness of those years that will never return, if not to torment them. All of them today look at the people who were yesterday with a critical and incredulous eye, with remorse, displeasure and, at times, despair. Then perhaps a tendentially re-socializing context, as the Constitution provides, necessarily re-educational, as Beccaria shouted in spite of what Kant and Hegel claimed, where there is the possibility of learning, maturing and understanding, makes these young people not different from any other person. There are those who can learn, mature and understand in the walls of their home, among school desks and with friends. On the other hand, there are those who suffered, felt unsuitable, refused and fought exclusion with the weapon of hatred. But these young people, taken and placed in an environment where they are taught something positive, are not so different from the others. There are, if anything, different moments in their life when they had the chance to understand. So the question is a moral obligation: if these disadvantaged, despised and suffering boys had had the opportunity to learn and understand first what they understood only after, paying the price for their choices, would it have been so simple to mislead them? Today Young Signorino, a young singer with millions of views on social media, a marketing phenomenon and self-proclaimed rapper, attributes the secret of his success to his genetic descent from Satan. The quality of his artistic talent matters little, the real lever is his self-proclamation as the son of the devil. What grips society is the charm of his character, built in the shadow of the antichrist. Satanism as a social lift, as a form of elevation which the young public inevitably undergoes charm. Too young to understand, to distinguish a cult from marketing: Young Signorino knows that to be successful, he must cling to this, while the young audience, in vain, falls into the illusion. And Satan becomes the key to success. Is society to blame? Is the Satanist a victim?

CHAPTER SIX

THE CRIME SCENE

"You know my method. It is founded upon the observation of trifles." (Arthur Conan Doyle, The Boscombe Valley Mystery)

Criminology is not an autonomous and self-sufficient discipline, but is part of many other sciences that deal with human nature and society. Indeed, any progress made in research into the causes of the crime must come from developments in these other branches of knowledge. Often too much time is wasted trying to find an elaborate and comprehensive definition of criminology, dividing and dividing its many branches of interest. At least twenty different terms are in use and form a confusing list: criminology, criminal science, criminal anthropology, criminal jurisprudence, criminal statistics, penology, prison science, penitentiary law, prison pedagogy, investigative science, crime and criminal profiling. It is not another definition that we need in this book, but a practical description of the functions. Take the heterogeneous composition of the population, the crowded urbanization of modern megacities, the intense mobility, the ever-growing temptations and opportunities, add new and disturbing dimensions to the crime phenomenon. Criminology must thus face modernity, the fragmentation of social connections and the "wear and tear of modern life". Through the disciplines related to crime, we will try to understand how to deal with crimes and crime scenes. All this in the next few pages, knowing full well that for each chapter dealt with, an entire monograph dedicated to exhausting the current topic would not suffice. Criminal psychology and investigative psychology can also be considered to belong to the criminal sciences, the former to the criminological sciences, and the latter to the forensic sciences. According to David Canter, founder of criminal and investigative psychology, psychology is directly applicable to the study of crime since crime must be viewed as a form of interpersonal relationship. In the case of the criminal act, this relationship is established between the criminal and the victim; therefore the modalities and motivations behind the criminal actions of a subject can be directly connected to those that accompany him in any other interpersonal relationship. One of the objectives of criminal and investigative psychology is to contribute to the definition of the so-called "psychological profile" of the possible author of a series of crimes, through a series of comparisons between investigative evidence (for example photographic findings) and psychological evidence- relational (the indicators of psychological and cognitive aspects of the person who committed the crime). This operation (which has become fashionable in many film and media productions, although it should be emphasized that there are not many real employment opportunities in the sector), is generally called criminal profiling (offender profiling or criminal profiling). The field of criminal profiling, beyond its media fame, also due to successful television series (see Mindhunter's success on Netflix) however, remains a sector that, despite the intensity of studies and research, has provided few satisfactory results. Criminology is often confused by the mass media with "criminalistics", or with crime investigation, even if they are very distinct sectors. While criminology is a science that studies crimes, offenders and possible measures to prevent, treat and control the crime, the investigation concerns activities aimed at finding out "who" has committed the crime in a specific way, put in place by the judicial police forces and by the defense of the suspect/accused of crimes, and criminalistics provide the same with the application methodologies for investigations, borrowed from the reference sciences (forensic sciences). Since the end of the nineteenth century, since the time of the discovery of fingerprints, criminalistics science has gone a long way. Today, for example, DNA analysis provides a new type of fingerprint, which allows to trace with remarkable levels of precision the identification of the perpetrator of some crimes. The chronicle shows that, more and more frequently, criminal cases are dealt with through sophisticated methodologies of investigation that draw from forensic sciences, that is, to those various disciplines that deal with the examination of traces found on the scene of a crime: forensic genetics , ballistics, toxicology, forensic medicine, electron microscopy. These sciences have nothing to do with criminology in a strict sense. In the process, these disciplines were increasingly relevant, often fundamental, to demonstrate the guilt of an offender or to exonerate an innocent person (also relative to distant and defined judicial facts); even if their claim to aspire to scientific "truth" has been repeatedly questioned by authoritative contributions. By entering with education and respect, but with a lot of curiosity, in the laboratories of modern criminalists, we will face another stage of this exciting journey into criminology. Are you ready? Let's begin. The crime scene can be any place, both indoors (e.g. a private home) and outdoors (e.g. a large shopping center). Each type of crime scene, together with the nature of the crime committed (robbery, murder, rape, arson, etc.) requires different investigation procedures. External crime scenes are the most problematic to investigate. Exposure to natural agents such as snow, rain, wind or heat, as well as to animal activity, contaminate the crime scene and lead to the destruction of evidence. Internal crime scenes are far less likely to be contaminated due to lack of exposure to the elements. Here, contamination usually occurs because of people: operators, onlookers and the same protagonists of the scene. At the crime scene, photos of all the evidence are taken before something is touched, moved or analyzed. Generally, numbered markers are placed near each test to allow the organization of the clues. Making a sketch of the crime scene is also a form of documentation. This allows investigators to take notes as well as measure distances and other information that may not be easily deduced from a photograph. Investigators will ascertain the location of the evidence and all other objects in the room. The sketch is usually drawn looking from above, which can also be useful like all other activities to obtain evidence. Generic diagnosis represents the first step, mandatory and indifferent, of the medical-legal laboratory investigation. Here, it is ascertained, for example, if a reddish spot is of a blood nature (i.e. if it is blood), if a yellowish consists of saliva, sperm or urine, if a fiber is natural (fragment of dress or hair) or artificial. Various tests are carried out for these checks. First guidelines or preliminary and, subsequently, tests of scientific certainty. The orientation tests are used as preliminary screening, being very sensitive (they are carried out with really small quantities of material), but not as specific. It is therefore necessary to carry out subsequent tests as well. The confirmation of the presence of blood, sperm, vaginal fluids, saliva, when possible, is obtained with techniques that give the certainty of the nature and the category the finding. These investigations are very reliable but have the disadvantage of requiring a fair amount of material, which can sometimes compromise subsequent identification investigations, which are extremely more sensitive. Generally speaking, there are four methods for determining the presence of blood or sperm:

- the visual method;

- the physical method;

- the chemical method;

- the microscopic method.

Apart from the visual method, each of these can give results of orientation or scientific certainty. The visual method, immediately and directly implemented, represents the preliminary phase which, even today, allows us to direct the search for traces to be subjected to subsequent laboratory tests. It should never be forgotten that the bloodstains can take on various color scales ranging from red to brown, up to dark green. Those of sperm from white to grayish, to yellowish, with edges typically "geographic", while those of saliva or sweat can be completely invisible macroscopically. The traces of sperm, but also of saliva, sweat, urine and other biological liquids, become visible in ultraviolet light or with the use of light sources at specific wavelengths, associated with appropriate lenses. They are of particular use when large surfaces have to be explored, with the result of making the spot appear luminescent. The microscopic examination assumes particular importance in the search for sperm, when the sperm cells whose characteristics are completely peculiar are highlighted. If there is a simple suspicion that on a substrate (e.g. an undergarment) there may be an invisible trace, it is possible to resort to chemical techniques that allow, in most cases, to detect its presence. Among the chemical methods for the blood nature, the tests based on the properties of the blood pigment should be mentioned. On a similar principle there are the tests that allow to detect the presence of even small quantities of blood because it is washed or very diluted (for example the catalytic test of Luminol), extremely sensitive, but also non-specific and, above all, their profiles of repeatability of the assessment are far from obvious. The generic diagnosis of saliva, however, is made through the demonstration of amylase in the trace. Amylase is an enzyme produced by pancreatic cells that promotes the digestion of food in the body. However, amylase is not only produced by the pancreas, but also by the salivary glands and, in women, by the fallopian tubes. For the diagnosis of feces, apart from the morphological and organoleptic characteristics, it is necessary to resort to tests that highlight the presence of urobilinogen or other faecal pigments. For the diagnosis of urine, apotryptophanase or tryptophanase is demonstrated with appropriate reagents or, more easily, by demonstrating the high concentration of urea and creatinine. Micro-crystallographic tests are also part of the chemical methods which consist in determining, through appropriate reagents, the formation of characteristic crystals both in the case of the blood stain (certainty test for the diagnosis of blood), and in that of sperm where, however, they do not allow the diagnosis of certainty, which is obtained instead with the microscopic investigation. Chromatographic tests on paper or on thin substrate can currently be considered the method of choice for the general diagnosis of blood, even on minimal traces.

"Science is the process that takes us from confusion to understanding..." (Brian Greene)

As for the investigations on hair, they are very frequent, given the ease with which this finding can be transferred from one place to another due to natural fall, to have been torn or to have remained on, for example, clothing. The investigations on hair, however, present problems similar to those relating to any other trace: that is, a generic, specific, individual, regional diagnosis may be required. The generic diagnosis is performed by observation with an optical microscope to detect the fundamental characteristics of the piliferous structure, i.e. the presence of a root, a stem and an end. Often, the limited amount of biological material available requires complex choices that can involve the sacrifice of the important preliminary step of generic diagnosis in favor of individual genetic diagnosis. Fact that realizes the apparent scientific paradox on the basis of which it is possible to identify with certainty a subject as "donor" of a track without it has been possible to establish the exact nature of the starting biological material. Once the nature of a stain has been identified, it is necessary to determine whether it is of human or animal nature (so-called diagnosis: species/specific). If the size of the trace allows it, the techniques still more used today for the diagnosis of species are immunological (immunodiffusion) which allow to compare an extract from the trace in question with different serums containing anti-human, anti-horse, dog antibodies , cat, etc. and to observe the formation of a band of precipitate in correspondence with the specific antiserum. Alternatively, methods that employ monoclonal antibodies against humans, dogs, cats, etc. are also commonly used with techniques aimed at the determination of antigens.

These techniques involve:

- Adhesion. A primary antibody is placed on the bottom of the plate well which will be the specific one for the antigen to be searched.

- Washing, to eliminate the antibodies that have not bound to the plate.

- The serum that should contain the antigen is added inside the well. If the antigen is present, this will bind with the primary antibody bound to the bottom of the plate.

- Washing, to eliminate the serum.

- Addition of a solution containing a secondary antibody that carries an enzyme bound. The secondary antibody will bind to the antigen (if this is present).

- Washing, to eliminate the secondary antibody that has not bound the antigen.

- Addition of a specific substrate for the enzyme linked to the secondary antibody. If the enzyme is present (and therefore the secondary antibody is present and therefore if the antigen is present) this will convert the substrate into a colored compound. The diagnosis of species on hair formations is generally performed by microscopic examination. In fact, the cuticle, i.e. the outer layer of the hair formation, the cortical substance, containing the pigment granules, and the medullary, i.e. the central portion that may be present, absent or in clods, have peculiar characteristics that easily allow the diagnosis of human or animal species. There are also more sophisticated genetic techniques, which provide for the examination of the mitochondrial DNA, also achievable on hair/hair; they are extremely sensitive and specific but have the disadvantage of invasiveness (and therefore the high cost), and are most often used not by forensic doctors but by zoologists. The question of the origin of a trace from a certain body district (regional diagnosis) concerns the piliferous formations and the traces of blood, since the generic diagnosis, for other biological materials, immediately identifies its origin. The regional morphological (macro/microscopic) diagnosis of hair, axillary hair, pubic hair, etc., based solely on the dimensional data (length, thickness) and on the shape of the section (round or oval), is far from providing elements of certainty. Various criteria apply to express general assessments regarding the origin of a blood spot: that is, we take into account the results of the somatic examination of the individual from whom the blood is said to originate, the characteristics of the site, of the amplitude, of the shape of the stains, and finally the microscopic examination of the material constituting them. Evidently, in order to have hemoptysis, respiratory tract injuries are required; to have a hemorrhoid hemorrhage, the existence of hemorrhoids is necessary; a woman who has passed menopause will not be able to attribute the spots to her own menstruation, etc. The location of the distribution of bloodstains, especially on clothing, as well as on bed linen, and elsewhere, can also be significant elements. More recent methods provide for the evaluation of tissue-specific gene expression by analyzing ribonucleic acid (RNA), which has unique characteristics for that specific tissue or cell type. A limitation of this analysis lies in the overall lower resistance of the RNA to degradation compared to the DNA: for this reason this approach may not allow any result on particularly scarce and/or degraded biological materials.

Forensic DNA

"The truth must be quite plain, if one could just clear away the litter." (Agatha Christie, A Caribbean Mystery)

We have all heard, at least once in a lifetime, of DNA profile (also called DNA fingerprinting, DNA testing, or DNA typing). DNA detection is a forensic technique used to identify individuals with characteristics of their DNA. A DNA profile is an agglomeration of variations of deoxyribonucleic or deoxyribonucleic acid that is different in all unrelated individuals, therefore being as unique to individuals as are fingerprints (hence the alternative name for the technique). The DNA profile should not be confused with complete genome sequencing. Developed from the beginning in 1985, the DNA profile is used, for example, for family tests and criminal investigations, to identify a person or to put a person in a crime scene; those techniques are now used globally in science forensics to facilitate police investigations and help clarify controversial paternity and immigration practices. The modern

DNA profiling process was developed in 1988 and increasingly perfected over time. Forensic medicine uses DNA, generally isolated from blood, skin, saliva, hair and other biological tissues and fluids, to identify those responsible for crimes or violence. The process used is genetic fingerprinting: this technique consists in comparing the length of the variable sections of the repetitive DNA, such as short tandem repeats and minisatellites, which can be very different between one individual and another. The comparison between two DNA samples under examination is therefore not based on the analysis of the entire deoxyribonucleotide sequence, but only on these sections. In fact, two individuals not related by kinship relationships have in common 99.9% of DNA sequence. This method is usually very reliable, although sometimes the identification of criminals can be complicated if the scene is contaminated by the DNA of several people. This method, developed in 1984 by British geneticist Sir Alec Jeffreys, was first used in 1988 to incriminate suspect Colin Pitchfork. In 1983, the body of a 15-year-old student, Lynda Mann, was found near Narborough, a small town in Leicestershire in the English Midlands. Lynda went to visit a friend of hers and never returned home. After two days the girl's body was found; it showed clear signs of strangulation and sexual violence. Police investigations led to nothing, but all the evidence was collected and cataloged, including biological evidence left by the murderer on the corpse. About three years later Dawn Ashworth, also a fifteen-year-old student, disappeared from home and was later found strangled and raped in the same wooded area where the previous murder had been committed. The girl had taken a shortcut from school instead of taking her usual route but, as the police suspected, her assailant, believing he had "got away" once, had committed the murder in the same way. Also in this case biological traces were collected on the corpse of the young student. The ways in which the violence and murder were perpetrated led the police to believe that they were the result of a single homicidal rapist. The police focused their suspicions on a young local man, Richard Buckland, a 17-year-old boy with learning difficulties, who had been spotted near Dawn Ashworth's murder scene. In addition, the boy appeared to be aware of details about the discovery of the girl's body, which the police had never revealed. After several interrogations, the young man confessed to the murder of the second girl, but denied any involvement in the murder three years earlier. At that point, the police requested the assistance of Sir Alec Jeffreys, an expert in DNA analysis. Jeffreys, at 09:05 on Monday 10 September 1984, had what the Anglo-Saxons call "eureka moment". In his laboratory in Leicester he faced an experiment and, looking at the image of a DNA film, he realized that it showed both the similarities and the differences between the DNA of different members of the family of one of his technicians. In about half an hour, he realized the possible scope of DNA as fingerprinting, which uses the variations in the genetic code of each individual. Jeffreys accepted the request and, in collaboration with the scientists of the British Forensic Science Service, compared the

DNA profiles obtained from the sperm samples taken from the crime scenes and the one obtained from a blood sample taken from the only suspect, and shortly after he handed over his results to the police. The two rapes were the result of one man's work, but this man was not Richard Buckland. A giant manhunt started in search of the subject whose genetic profile corresponded to that of the violence. All adult male individuals in the area were asked to spontaneously donate a sample of their blood for comparison. Obviously a refusal would have attracted the police suspects and therefore about 5000 blood samples were analyzed. However, even this enormous effort was useless and no trace of the murderer was found. It was then assumed that the killer was not resident in those areas, but an individual passing through. Just when all hopes of finding the culprit seemed to have vanished, a witness said he heard a man in a pub bragging that he had provided a blood sample instead of a friend, Colin Pitchfork, who had asked him for a favor. Colin Pitchfork was a young baker in the village, and had asked his friend for the favor, because being he on bail for a conviction for obscene acts, he said, he would certainly have been accused and framed by the Police. He managed to convince his friend that he had nothing to do with the deaths of the two girls. The police immediately went to him and collected his DNA. His genetic profile was the same as those obtained from both crime scenes. Pitchfork confessed to both murders, telling the most heinous details. But who was Colin Pitchfork? He was a married man, father of two children, and was twenty-three years old at the time of the events. Before his marriage, he had been convicted of obscene acts and was in therapy at a hospital center. He worked as a baker, and was particularly skilled as a sculptor of cake decorations and for this he was highly esteemed in the town, especially by children. His boss claimed that he was: "a very good worker, who met deadlines but had to be kept from working with female staff because he was a little moody". During the interrogation he admitted that he had a sort of "compulsion" towards women, which was manifested to him when he was only a boy and this pushed him to commit obscene acts. Even in the case of the two girls, they ran away when he had approached them and this had excited him, then he killed them for fear of being reported. Young Buckland and the baker Pitchfork were the first two suspects to experiment with the use of the DNA profile in a courtroom. The first, seeing his innocence demonstrated, the second, seeing his guilt definitively proven. In 1988 Colin Pitchfork was sentenced to life imprisonment, with a sentence of thirty years for the violence and murder of the two girls. In current practice, suspects are often asked to provide a DNA sample for comparison with any biological findings present at the crime scene. Furthermore, sad news in these times of international terrorism, genetic fingerprinting can also be used to identify the victims of mass accidents. In terms of DNA, there is a particular forensic extraction procedure. In fact, in order to be analyzed, the DNA must be extracted from the trace or the reference sample and purified from the proteins and substances that may have been present on it (e.g. dust, soil, fibers of clothing, etc.). The step of determining the quantity and quality of the extracted DNA is necessary in order to be able to adjust the quantity necessary for the subsequent phases, now carried out almost exclusively by means of the chain polymerization reaction (PCR) technique. The study of DNA polymorphisms in the forensic field is carried out by comparing genetic structures. For example, the profile of the DNA extracted from the blood trace present on the suspect's pants with that extracted from the blood of the victim, or the profile of the DNA extracted from the seminal fluid taken from the victim of sexual violence with that of a possible investigated person. The result that derives from this can be of complete discrepancy between two genetic structures, or of compatibility, but not of identity. The question that is usually asked of the forensic geneticist is whether a certain individual can be excluded as the one who left the trace on the crime scene. While, as mentioned, the answer to the first part of the question can be very quick, due to the complete incompatibility between two genetic profiles, the answer to the second is not as simple. And, on this aspect, the cases of judicial reporting have spent many words. An answer to this question, in fact, passes through an evaluation of the frequency in the reference population (Italian, Dutch, English, etc.) of the phenotype (genotype), obtained from the examination of each system which leads to a cumulative frequency value, which in turn reveals the greater or lesser rarity of the profile. The reciprocal of this frequency value represents the number of subjects in the reference population who randomly share the same genetic profile. Values of 1 in 10,000, 1 in 100,000 are rapidly giving way to extremely more significant values, such as those of 1 out of several billion or more, thanks to the possibility of using increasingly informative genetic systems, or with very low cumulative frequencies. Therefore, in carrying out the investigations, the genetic systems used, i.e. those with greater discriminative capacity than others, are of fundamental importance. The DNA test, for several years now, has proven to be completely reliable and usable even in delicate investigations in the forensic field, provided that the relevant quality standards are respected through the guidelines and directives that at various levels are issued by international and national scientific communities. The goal of maximum reliability is achieved through a specific preparation of those who work there (laboratory managers, technicians, etc.), through suitable structures and machinery, and also through the use of operating techniques that have the approval of the international scientific community: the genetic systems used, in fact, must prove to be sufficiently reliable, informative, transmissible according to the rules of Mendelian segregation (relative to the use in paternity investigations) and must be accompanied by an adequate set of frequency data in the population.

Weapons and forensic ballistics

"It is the care we bestow on apparently trifling, unatractive and very troublesome minutiae which determines the result." (William Ian Beardmore Beveridge, The Art of Scientific Investigation)

Forensic ballistics is based on the principle that all firearms are characterized by indelible, unique differences, due to the heterogeneous mechanism with which they are manufactured. Forensic ballistics represents a link between the science of the motion of a bullet, or that particular branch of physics with links to mathematics, chemistry and law (Criminal Process, Criminal Law and Criminal Procedure). In cases where a firearm has been used, with consequent injuries or death, a correct medical-legal diagnosis, although based on the careful examination of the "basic" data (number of shots exploded, firing distance and mutual position between the victim and the victim), may sometimes prove incomplete or insufficient in the absence of an integrated assessment with the results of investigations commonly considered to be of a more exquisitely criminal nature: the examination of the weapon and its mechanics, the definition of the number of shots unexploded in the magazine, identification of the caliber of the exploded projectiles, and interpretation of environmental and testimonial findings. The forensic ballistics investigations for the identification and description of the place where the event occurred; the examination of damage by ballistic agent in environments and on vehicles; the search, collection, conservation and identification of the finds of ballistic interest; examination of the weapon, verification of its characteristics and functionality; identification of the shooter; firing distance evaluation. In addition to these, in proposing reconstructive hypotheses of the event, due consideration should be given to the medico-legal issues regarding the assessment of the time of death and/or injury, the cause and the means used, such as example survival time and the possibility of autonomously carrying out actions or displacements after injury, type or types of weapon used, caliber, number of shots, firing distance and mutual position between victim and shooter. However, forensic ballistics suffers from certain difficulties of analysis with particular types of weapons whose projectiles flow through plastic patinas which prevent their contact with the barrel. For this type of weapon there are other analyzes that can reveal its sources. In cases where a firearm has been used, resulting in injury or death of the act, a (correct) medical-legal diagnosis, although based on the careful examination of the "basic factual" data (number of shots exploded views, shooting distance and mutual position between actor and victim), can often prove incomplete or non-exhaustive. This is true in cases where there is an absence of an evaluation accompanied by investigations commonly considered to be of a more exquisitely criminal nature, such as: the examination of the weapon and its mechanics, the definition of the number of unexploded shots in the magazine, identification of the caliber of the exploded projectiles, as well as the interpretation of environmental and testimonial findings. Forensic ballistics therefore means everything that has in any way to do with the attempted or actual use, direct or indirect, of a firearm. The weapon in question may be known or not. We too, for didactic - scientific and exhibition reliability, have classified the areas of competence of the ballistic investigation into four categories: "internal ballistics"; "analysis of weapons in general"; "technology analysis" and "motion of the bullets inside the barrel". Internal ballistics analyzes the transformation of the chemical energy of a powder into mechanical energy (mainly kinetic), due to the propulsion of a projectile. Internal ballistics studies the phenomena that occur from the moment the cartridge is fired until the moment the bullet comes out of the weapon's mouth. The next phase, as mentioned above, becomes the object of study of external ballistics. Following the violent action of the firing pin on the trigger capsule, the primer composition is compressed against the anvil of the capsule (in the case of annular percussion, the trigger is crushed against the metal of the bottom edge). The composition detonates producing an intense blazing lightning that, through the holes of the trigger, reaches the charge of dust, giving way to its explosion. This will be more or less fast in relation to the priming force, the type, conformation and quantity of the powder, the loading density (ratio between the volume of the powder and the space in the cartridge), the compression exerted on the powder, the force with which the bullet is held by the cartridge case and many other variables. The dust must be able to completely burn before the bullet comes out of the barrel, both because in this way all the energy is used, and to prevent the residues from igniting outside the muzzle of the weapon (blaze of muzzle). External ballistics deals with the analysis of the motion of the projectile in the external space between the muzzle of the weapon and the target or the point of fall. In the external space the projectile follows a trajectory which is the result of three distinct forces: the initial impulse which gives it a uniform and straight motion, the resistance of the air which opposes it in the opposite direction, and the force of gravity which tends to drop the bullet towards the ground with uniformly accelerated motion. Air resistance plays an important role for fast projectiles and therefore, for very slow projectiles (ancient artillery, arrows, stones) it can be almost neglected. Think, in a purely exemplifying sense, that for a nineteenth-century mortar the difference compared to the trajectory in the void was only 10%. External ballistics therefore analyzes the "conduct" and trajectory of all bodies launched into space up to their point of impact; it includes the measurement and calculation of the velocity of the bullet at the exit from the barrel. What does terminal ballistics do instead? It deals with the analysis of the effects of bullets, cartridge elements, fragments and splinters on the animated target (man and animal) or on inanimate raw material. Terminal ballistics therefore analyzes the "behavior" of the bullet when it reaches the target and the consequent physiological and biological reactions in the affected living body. In other words, terminal ballistics studies the behavior of the bullet in the target. One of the phenomena that best lends itself to a scientific study is that of the penetration of the projectile into the various media, while considering that the diversity of materials and the diversity of behavior of the individual projectiles, according to their structure and speed at the moment of impact, do not allow the use of a general mathematical model, but only empirical formulas. That is to concrete cases, which can be analyzed from time to time. It happens in fact, on one hand, that high-speed projectiles are easily deformed on impact and, on the other hand, that very fast projectiles do not have time to transfer their energy to the target! Fundamental, in this field of forensic study, is the autopsy aimed at determining the causes and methods of the death of the victim, estimating the shooting distance, the dynamics of the crime event; for this reason it is absolutely necessary, as well as good practice, that the forensic doctor be assisted by an expert in forensic ballistics. The "ballistics of injuries" is also of considerable importance for the coroner, for the ballistic expert and for the criminalist, in the analysis of some crimes and the understanding of the related harmful phenomena, in order to deny or confirm hypotheses and testimonies and to carry out a scientific reconstruction of the dynamics of the crime event. Terminal ballistics also plays an important role in the construction of fireproof protections (armoring of vehicles, construction of Kevlar bulletproof vests, etc.). Given this premise, let's try to sketch a conclusion and an overall look at the matter. Internal, external and terminal ballistics merge and materialize in the broad theoretical-operational field of the so-called identification ballistics. This science deals, among other things, with analysis, technical evaluation and microscopic comparison of ballistic finds, with the identification and study of the weapon used in a criminal event starting from the exact metric-morphological data of ballistic finds found on the crime scene. It also deals with the decoding of the marks of the weapons and the reconstruction of the worn or obliterated registration marks, and the analysis of the GSR shot residues following the deflagration of a cartridge. But that's not all, the identification ballistics addresses the estimation of the firing distance starting from both the evaluation of the density of any shot residues found on certain subjects and/or their clothing and from the analysis of the terminal ballistic lesions on the victim and the ballistic characteristics of the weapon used. It also deals with the dynamics of the event and the examination of the crime scene, the computerized three-dimensional reconstruction of the crime scene and the dynamics of the crime event in order to identify the epicentres of fire, the trajectories of the bullets and the reciprocal positions (shooter - victim - eyewitnesses) so as to scientifically succeed in denying or confirming hypotheses and testimonials and much more. Investigations on gunshot residues are also included in this area.

"Blackstone's Police Operational Handbook recommends the ABC of serious investigation: Assume nothing, Believe nothing, and Check everything." (Ben Aaronovitch, Moon Over Soho)

It is an intriguing and fascinating science, very technological, still evolving both on the interpretation of data and on the research itself that deals with it. The illustrious scholar Gonzales in the 1930s was the first to take an interest in and establish a particular method for identifying the gunshot residues on the suspect's hands. He identified a procedure that involved the spreading of melted paraffin, therefore very hot, on the hands of the suspects. The fact that it was very hot should have, in theory, dilated the pores of the suspect's epidermis and captured any particles present on the hand, both burned and unburned. The final cooled product, called paraffin glove, was subjected to a chemical investigation called Diphenylamine. The end result of this research, in the case of positivity, was that the residues were colored blue. However, it was then shown that this coloring was achieved also in the presence of urine (nitrites and nitrates) and fertilizers, etc. During investigations into the murder of President Kennedy in the United States, methods were developed to ascertain the presence of metal residues resulting from the detonation of the priming mixture: lead styphnate, barium dioxide, antimony sulfide, etc. technical research guidelines. In the forensic world, and more generally in the scientific universe, even a few years can lead to major changes. Two important events in this area are briefly reported below. On February 15, 2007, the ASTM (standard specification) approved a new release of the GSR standard called E 1588. In addition to numerous other changes compared to the previous version, one of the most significant innovations was the definitive de-classification of compatible features. In October of the same year, the 15th

International Forensic Science Symposium organized by Interpol was held in Lyon. In this congress the criteria and guidelines already established during the F.B.I. Symposium of 2005 and some other works published by researchers in the meantime. For professionals, this means that an important change has occurred in the operating techniques, protocols and evaluation of the results obtained. An important element of probative validity for the purpose of identifying the offender, where a firearm has been used, is the search for the residuals of the shot. The interest attributed to this means of investigation is of considerable technical relevance as the science itself is reduced to types of assessments considered insecure, doubtful and quarrelsome that did not allow, in fact, to ascertain in "science and consciousness" the presence or absence of particles resulting from the deflagration of ammunition. During the firing of a firearm, the considerable pressure and temperature of the combustion gases inside the barrel, on one hand, causes the projectile to escape, while on the other it causes chemical-physical reactions on very small particles of gunpowder. The latter are projected out of the same weapon and invest the surrounding surfaces in the form of aerosols. Generally speaking, in the cartridges there are two types of gunpowder: the trigger powder that transforms the mechanical energy of percussion into thermo-chemical energy, which is subsequently transferred to the launch powder: the launch powder that creates the bullet propulsion. As components of the trigger it is customary to find: barium, nitrate, lead, calcium, silicide, antimony, sulphide etc. The material most commonly used for the manufacture of the cartridge cases is brass Cu-Zn 35 (the number indicates the percentage of zinc present). Aluminum, zinc, copper and some types of plastics are also used in the manufacturing of the cases. As far as bullets are concerned, they can consist of only lead, or have the central part (core) in lead and an external coating (shell) in copper or antimony or nickel. The residues of the shot, therefore, can be constituted not only by elements coming from the triggers, but also by those that derive from the external coating of the bullet and from the edge of the cartridge case.

When the deflagration takes place inside the combustion chamber of a weapon, three phases occur in a few seconds. A first phase (so-called pyrostatic) characterized by the combustion of the throwing powder at a constant volume, since the projectile is stationary. In this phase, the temperature reaches 2,000°C and the pressure reaches 1,400 p.s.i. (pound square inch = pound x square inch); a second phase (so-called pyrodynamics), characterized by the contemporaneity of constant volume combustion and variable pressures. The temperature and pressure reach the maximum levels: around 3,600 ° C and around 40,000 p.s.i. A final and third phase (so-called expansion) characterized by the expansion of the gas and the motion of the projectile. The three phases occur almost simultaneously with the detonation of the trigger. As already mentioned, metallic elements such as iron, antimony and barium, which are part of the chemical composition of the trigger powders, during firing (as well as other metallic elements which are part of the chemical composition of the throwing powder, due to the high thermal and mechanical energy and the high pressure to which they are subjected) undergo a process of fusion and subsequent vaporization, thus finding themselves present together in the form of melted droplets (aerosols) which immediately cool down coming to often, but not always, take on a characteristic spheroidal appearance, similar to the phenomenon of volcanic boluses; that's way they have been called fireballs. The shape and composition of these residues, called **GSR** (Gun Shot Residue) or **CDR** (Cartridge Discharge Residue), which come from the priming powder during the shot, is such as to leave no doubt for investigation purposes. In fact, human activities other than firing that can produce particles containing lead (Pb), barium (Ba) and antimony (Sb) are not known at present. Their diameter usually ranges from 0.5 to 50 microns. Persistence times are important elements for identification, interpretation and conclusions. Due to the force of gravity, the number of particles present on a given surface is destined to decrease over time. We are talking about the relationship between the number of hours and the number of particles. It is evident that the use of the various types of weapons necessarily affects the quantity of particles present on the person under investigation (short weapon, long weapon, etc.). The shape and diameter are very influential for the conclusions. For example, finding a large particle after a time span of many hours is a negative element, precisely because the large particles are the first to fall due to the force of gravity.

Fingerprints and dactyloscopy

"You don't have to believe in coincidences because they happen every day. The trick is to be able to discern when something is more than coincidence." (Glenn Jones, Introduction to Intelligence Analysis - work in progress)

The skin that covers the entire human body, the epidermis, is made up of five layers from the inside to the outside of the body, characterized by a greater state of keratinization: stratum basale, stratum spinosum, stratum granulosum, stratum lucidum, and stratum corneum. The basal or germinativum layer is composed of small and very thickened cells, arranged in palisade on the membrane in contact with the dermis. The cells of this layer reproduce and are pushed towards the surface to form the next layer, which is called "spiny" or "Malpighi". Said layer is formed by coarsely polyhedral shaped cells, more flattened than those of the basal layer and separated from each other by intercellular substance. The surfaces of the palms of the hands, the soles of the feet and the inside of the phalanges, are characterized by a particular structure such as the dermal papillae, which determine the formation of the skin crests, which are small fleshy reliefs that contain the Messner's tactile corpuscles. The papillae, which reach the outermost surface, have tiny sweat pores that secrete a transparent substance composed of water, sodium chloride, potassium carbonate, volatile fatty acids, sulphates, etc., so, if the skin crests come into contact with a more or less smooth surface, they deposit the substance secreted by them, determining the formation of an impression, mirroring their design. A fingerprint is a trace left by the dermatoglyphs of the last phalanx of the fingers. A dermatoglyph is instead the result of the alternation of ridges and furrows. Dermatoglyphs are present on the palms of the hands, on the soles of the feet and on the fingertips. The crests vary in width from 100 to 300 microns, while the furrow period corresponds to approximately 500 microns. Dactyloscopy is the branch of criminalistics that studies papillary skin crests, mainly of the fingertips, in order to identify the offender, based on the prints left by him at the crime scene. It should be noted that the application of dactyloscopy to identify the offender allows for an indirect search for identity, which is obviously relative and not absolute. The mathematician Balthazard established a system of recognition and comparison of the fingerprints which was based on an exponential type of empirical formula; he hypothesized that between two fingerprints there could have been just seventeen points of correspondence, on a series of seventeen billion one hundred seventy-nine million (17,179,000,000) of specimens! In practice, a possibility out of tens of billions that a fingerprint fragment, containing seventeen characteristic marks, may have been deposited by a person other than that to which it is attributed: if we consider that the world population is only a few billion individuals however, distributed over the entire surface of the globe, this occurrence can reasonably be considered at least unlikely. A statistically improbable event does not necessarily have to be considered impossible with absolute certainty. However, in the case of fingerprints, the differentiating elements are such and so many, that an unlikely event can practically be considered impossible. Two fingerprints left by the same individual will never be perfectly superimposable; in fact, the identity between two fingerprints is determined not by the perfect overlap, but by the coincidence of the shape of the papillary bundles and by a high number of points of detail. Fragments of fingerprints, even very small, would provide numerous elements of evidence if we used poroscopy, suggested by Edmond Locard, which is based on the examination of the pores of the fingertip crests. Poroscopy is the last frontier of the papillary investigation and allows us to uniquely identify a trace from the morphology of the pore on the epidermis. It is evident, in fact, that in a fingerprint the quantity of identifiable identification points is proportional to the surface that can be examined: the smaller it is, the less likely it is to ascertain a sufficient number of particularities on it, or to obtain identification of the person to whom it belongs. The application of poroscopy, i.e. the study of the position of the sweat pores, would lead to a significant reduction in the minimum area necessary for identification tests. The first court case that was solved thanks to the fingerprints of the culprit dates back to about a century ago. The fingertips and palms of our hands (and also of the feet) are sprinkled with tiny conical shaped papillae that follow one after the other forming thin crests separated by small furrows. The crests describe characteristic, absolutely individual designs (lugs, arches, vortices), that two monovular twins have the same DNA, but different fingerprints. The papillary crests are formed during the twelfth week and are completed after the sixth month of intrauterine life; they are also preserved in corpses, as long as epidermal support exists. The papillary crests do not undergo transformations over the life of an individual, except in special cases, in which they themselves constitute salient marks for the identification of a person. The fingerprints are different from individual to individual and, in the same individual, the traces left by the ten fingers are all different from each other. On the classifiability of fingerprints, which can be traced back to the four basic types of figure, namely delta, monodelta, bidelta and mixed. The papillary designs, in fact, do not alter their morphology during the individual's life, that is, they remain unchanged from the moment of their formation, around the third month of intrauterine life, until the onset of putrefactive phenomena following death, except in the case of traumatic effects (for example, deep removal of the dermis), or following particular infectious skin diseases. The epidermis is layered on the dermatoglyphs contained on the lower layers of the dermis and therefore fingerprints are also reconstructed in case of lesions on the skin.

Elements of forensic archeology

"Supposing is good, but finding out is better." (Mark Twain)

In less than a hundred years, the classic figure of the archaeologist has changed radically. In fact, the modern "Indiana Jones" have specialized more and more, appropriating techniques and applications pertinent to multiple scientific disciplines, serving them to their needs. Forensic archeology is a sector of judicial archeology that concerns the use of reading techniques and interpretation of the material traces and contexts of the archaeological discipline in the medical-legal field. The forensic archaeologist deals in particular in the analysis of a crime scene for the recognition and classification of the finds, the identification of their origin and era, and for the reconstruction of the spatial arrangement of people or objects in a given place and moment and the temporal sequence of anthropic and natural actions occurred. The acquisition of new scientific techniques applied to archeology has allowed the archaeologist to work also in the forensic field, making his specialization available to investigators both in contexts related to crime scenes, and to those related to other areas such as mass accidents (for example due to plane crashes) or cases of mass burials. The first state to employ archaeologists to search for human remains was the United Kingdom: in 1988 the discovery of the body of a minor, Stephen Jennings, by a team of forensic archaeologists, in fact marked the beginning of a close collaboration between investigating authorities and forensic archaeologists in cadaveric concealment scenarios. Forensic archeology is now called to answer questions relating to the concealment of bodies, weapons, drugs, stolen goods, etc. and identification and possible excavation in the event of mass burials in wartime. The illustrious scientist John Hunter was the first author who in "Forensic Archeology: Advances in Theory and Practice" (2001) exposed the questions to which the competence of the forensic archaeologist can give answers. In Europe and in the world the presence of the forensic archaeologist is generally required in two cases: **1.** excavation of an underground burial discovered accidentally;

2. targeted research, following judicial police investigations, and in case of discovery, excavation of a burial. When human remains are found ("clandestine burial"), the presence of a forensic doctor and, in the case of skeletal remains, the forensic anthropologist are also required. The archaeologist will therefore have to stop all excavation operations until the arrival of the latter with whom he will have to work in a team under the direction of a public prosecutor. In case of concealment of a buried corpse immediately after death, by excavating archaeologically, a series of investigations may be carried out to establish the period to which the underground tomb dates. The stratigraphic sciences, in which archaeologists are experts, will be able to provide indications on the terminus ante quem by analyzing the layers that cover the pit, and on the terminus post quem by analyzing the stratigraphy cut by the underground tomb and the material inside. In fact, in case of superficial fortuitous discoveries, it is not always obvious that it is a corpse buried inside a pit. This is why it is necessary to consult a forensic archaeologist, so that his correct reading of the stratigraphic sequence of the soil can determine if we are in the presence of an old tomb, a hidden corpse, or something else.

The preservation of the integrity of the burial carried out by the forensic anthropologist (specialized in the preservation of the finds) will allow the coroner and the anthropologist to perform a detailed examination of the body on the site of the discovery, provided that the original configuration of the corpse has not been compromised by the excavation. In conclusion, the relationship between science and law is a fascinating and at the same time insidious and complex thing. It is not a question of sterile and purely theoretical importance, but of events which have their practical repercussions and which concern the lives of many people. Just think of the decisions that a magistrate makes on the basis of the so-called "scientific evidence".

The forensic sciences are nothing but the set of a broad spectrum of scientific disciplines applied to the field of law. The term "forensic science" is so vast, in fact, that includes an infinite number of scientific disciplines. But it is in the methods and objectives that science and law differ dramatically. Science aims to achieve the objective, authentic truth. The law, however, more prosaically, is satisfied with the "procedural" truth. In the courts, in fact, a judge or a jury establishes what the "truth" is, and truth lies in what they themselves deliberate, that is the "procedural truth". Despite this, those involved in forensic science know that team work with other experts (investigators, magistrates, lawyers, etc.) is essential to bring the truth closer and serve justice

BIBLIOGRAPHY

American Psychiatric Association, DSM-5. Manuale diagnostico e statistico dei disturbi mentali, Raffaello Cortina Editore, 2014

Barresi F. (2000) Sette religiose criminali. Dal satanismo criminale ai culti distruttivi, Ed. Up. Blanchot M. (2003) Lautreamont e Sade, SE.

Barresi F., Sette religiose criminali, EdUP Roma, 2006

Bellaspiga L., Il caso Finale Emilia. Abusi solo presunti ma vite distrutte. «Processi da rifare», in Avvenire, 7 gennaio 2018.

Boffi E., La strage degli innocenti della Bassa Modenese. Cronaca di un processo diabolico, in Tempi, 21 dicembre 2014.

Boffi E., I pedofili e satanisti della Bassa Modenese non erano né pedofili né satanisti. Così hanno ammazzato una comunità cattolica, su Tempi, 5 dicembre 2014.

Brunetta N., Il satanismo nelle aule giudiziarie, Edizioni Segno, 2011

Bruschi V., Modena, un figlio dei Covezzi: "Voglio conoscere i miei fratelli", Il Resto del Carlino, 15 febbraio 2017.

Cantelmi T., Cacace C., Il libro nero del satanismo, Edizioni San Paolo, 2007

Cerasa C., Ho visto l'uomo nero: L'inchiesta sulla pedofilia a Rignano Flaminio tra dubbi, sospetti e caccia alle streghe, LIT

EDIZIONI, 30 settembre 2007

Chasseguet Smirgel J. (1987) Creatività e perversione, Raffaello Cortina.

Crowley A., The book of the law, Red Wheel/Weiser, 2004

De Masi F. (1999) La perversione sadomasochistica. L'oggetto e le teorie, Bollati Boringhieri.

Di Nola A. M. (1980) Il diavolo. Le manifestazioni del demoniaco nella storia fino ai nostri giorni, Scipione.

Freud S. (1908) La morale sessuale civile e il nervosismo moderno OSF, Boringhieri, 1972.

Freud S. (1919) Un bambino viene picchiato. In: Opere, Vol.8. Boringhieri, Torino, 1976.

Freud S. (1922) Una nevrosi demoniaca nel secolo decimo settimo, in O. S. F., Bollati Boringhieri, 1977, IX.

Goldberg A. (1995) The problem of perversion, Yale University Press, New Haven.

Hirigoyen M.F. (2000) Molestie morali. La violenza perversa nella famiglia e nel lavoro, Einaudi.

Introvigne M., Indagine sul Satanismo. Satanisti a antisatanisti dal seicento ai nostri giorni, cit., p. 293.

Introvigne M., The Church of Scientology, ELLEDICI, Leumann (TO), 1998, p. 5.

Introvigne M., I satanisti. Storia, riti e miti del satanismo, SugarCo,

2010

Introvigne M., Il cappello del mago, SugarCo, 1996

Jones E. (1912) Psicologia dell'incubo [Tit. orig.: Der Alptraum in seiner Beziehung zu gewissen Formen des mittelalterlichen Aberglaubens, in Schriften zur Angewandten Seelenkunde, XIV (7),] Newton Compton, 1978.

Jung C. G. (1948) L'io e l'inconscio, Einaudi, 1948.

Kernberg O. (1996) Aggressività, disturbi della personalità e perversioni, Cortina Raffaello.

LaVey A., The Satanic Bible, Avon Books, 1969

LaVey A., The Satanic Rituals, HarperCollins, 1976

Meltzer D. (1973) Stati sessuali della mente, Armando Editore.

Milton J. (2006) Paradiso perduto, Oscar Classici Mondadori.

Perrotta G., Criminologia esoterica. Manule di studio teorico-pratico, Primiceri Editore, 2016

Rank O. (1914) Il Doppio [Tit. orig.: Der Doppelgünger, in Imago, III, 1914] SugarCo, 1967.

Stoller R. (1978) Perversione. La forma erotica dell'odio, Feltrinelli.

Strano M. (2003) Manuale di Criminologia clinica, See Edizioni.

Treccani, vocabolario di lingua italiana, s.v. "esoterico"

Trincia P. e Rafanelli A., Episodio 2: La casa di via Abba Motto

19, in Veleno, la Repubblica.

Zipparri (200) Nel Nome del Padre e di Edipo. Appunti di psicoanalisi e religione per il nuovo millennio, Armando Editore.

SITOGRAPHY:

http://docplayer.it/12731536-Rapporto-sul-satanismo-in-italia-aggiornato-agosto-2007.html

https://xeper.org/

www.adnkronos.com

www.altrarealta.com

www.bambinidisatana.com/

www.churchofsatan.com/

www.churchofsatan.com/interview-washington-post-magazine.php

www.cinquantamila.it

www.corrieredellasera.it

www.dailycases.com

www.intercom-sf.com

www.ilgiorno.it

www.oto.org/

www.quotidiano.net

www.repubblica.it

www.reteluna.it

www.ristretti.org

---

[1]   Alchemy is an esoteric science that involves different disciplines (astrology, chemistry, physics, metallurgy and medicine) and that was born with the aim of transforming lead, a metaphor for all that is negative, into gold, that is, all that is positive, to reach perfection and find your own inner God.

[2]   Voodoo is an African American religion still widespread today. It was associated with Satanism and therefore condemned by the church for the similarity of some rites and beliefs, such as animal sacrifices, the ritualistic importance of blood and animals that Christians consider evil (for example snakes), possessions and black magic.

[3]   The cabal is an esoteric Jewish doctrine, which studies and interprets the Bible by explaining the relationship between the universe, the human being and nature in order to achieve spiritual fulfillment.

[4]   Numerology is the discipline that seeks a correlation between numbers (dates, quantities of vowels or consonants present in a name, etc.) and characteristics of real objects and situations.

[5]   While white magic is considered beneficial, in which the person lives in harmony with nature and intervenes for the sole purpose of achieving health, prosperity and benefits for himself and for others; black magic includes a set of rituals, formulas and spells that the magician performs to gain control of dark and supernatural forces in order to cause harm to others.

[6]   Very famous in Italy is the Noce of Benevento

[7]   It seems that the human fat used for these candles was supplied by the royal executioners.

[8]   http://www.oto.org/

[9]   http://www.intercom-sf.com/modules.php?name=News&file=article&sid=365.%20Visitato%20il%2003.%2008.%202009

[10]   Massimo Introvigne, Il satanismo, ELLEDICI, Leumann (TO), 1998, p.19

[11]   Massimo, Introvigne, Indagine sul satanismo. Satanisti ed anti-

satanisti dal 600 ai giorni nostri, cit., p.261.

[12]   The sign of the horns is a reference to the Devil as the index and pinkie finger that remain raised recall his horns, and the three lowered fingers deny the Christian Trinity.

[13]   http://www.churchofsatan.com/interview-washington-post-magazine.php

[14]   https://xeper.org/

[15]   "As the twentieth century draws to a close, the Church of Scientology has emerged as one of the most important chapters of the ongoing controversy over new religions and the rise of religious pluralism in the West. The teachings of the founder, L. Ron Hubbard, had some measure of immediate success after their first public presentation in 1950, but at the time it would have been difficult to predict the overwhelming rise of Scientology or the history of its controversies, if we had limited ourselves to examining its beginnings, all in all modest. Controversy over Scientology has affected almost all aspects of the Church and its founder." Massimo Introvigne, The Church of Scientology, ELLEDICI, Leumann (TO), 1998, p. 5.

[16]   Massimo Introvigne, Indagine sul Satanismo. Satanisti a antisatanisti dal seicento ai nostri giorni, cit., p. 293.

[17]   DSM stands for Diagnostic and Statistical Manual of Mental Disorders. It is the manual that collects all known mental disorders, used by doctors, psychiatrists and psychologists from all over the world. It is periodically updated. Today the most updated version is the fifth edition.

[18]   We will discuss this better in the third chapter

[19]   These women are called «breeders»

[20]   Quotidiano.Net, "Noi, plagiati per inventare abusi". Marta: così fui strappata a mamma, su Quotidiano.Net, 1542188647304.

[21]   Pablo Trincia e Alessia Rafanelli, Episodio 2: La casa di via Abba Motto 19, in Veleno, la Repubblica.

[22]   Emanuele Boffi, La strage degli innocenti della Bassa Modenese. Cronaca di un processo diabolico, in Tempi, 21 dicembre 2014.

[23]   Emanuele Boffi, I pedofili e satanisti della Bassa Modenese non erano né pedofili né satanisti. Così hanno ammazzato una comunità cattolica, su Tempi, 5 dicembre 2014.

[24]   Viviana Bruschi, Modena, un figlio dei Covezzi: "Voglio conoscere i miei fratelli", Il Resto del Carlino, 15 febbraio 2017.

[25]   Claudio Cerasa, Ho visto l'uomo nero: L'inchiesta sulla pedofilia a Rignano Flaminio tra dubbi, sospetti e caccia alle streghe, LIT EDIZIONI, 30 settembre 2007, ISBN 978-88-6826-534-2.

[26]   Lucia Bellaspiga, Il caso Finale Emilia. Abusi solo presunti ma vite distrutte. «Processi da rifare», in Avvenire, 7 gennaio 2018.

[27]   http://www.churchofsatan.com/

[28]   http://docplayer.it/12731536-Rapporto-sul-satanismo-in-italia-aggiornato-agosto-2007.html

[29]   https://www.bambinidisatana.com/

[30]   The Demiurge is a philosophical and mythological figure, introduced by Plato in Timaeus, who orders the cosmos and gives soul to the matter.

[31]   According to the definition of DSM-V paraphilias are "all those atypical sexual behaviors for which the subject feels a strong and persistent erotic-sexual arousal."

[32]   Saraceno C., Naldini M., The sociology of family, Il Mulino, 2013

[33]   An example of a "textbook" religious sect is Scientology.

[34]   Art. 21, VI paragraph: "Printed publications, shows and all other manifestations contrary to morality are prohibited. The law lays down adequate measures to prevent and suppress violations."

[35]   Constitutional Court, sentence no. 9 of 1965.

[36]   *Raccomandazione 05 febbraio 1992, n. 1178*, http://www.olir.it/documenti/?documento=1257

[37]   Recommendation 22 June 1999, n. 1396, http://www.dimarzio.info/en/articles/institutions/48 recommendation-1396-1999-religion-and-democracy.html

[38]   http://www.antiplagio.it/

[39]   In criminology the dark number indicates all those crimes and deviant phenomena which, by not being reported, do not compose the official statistics and whose authors remain unknown and unpunished. Knowing that there is an obscure number, in relation to certain social phenomena that are difficult to monitor, allows scholars not to base their deductions only on the objective reality that results from the analyzes, since the phenomenon would be described incorrectly both qualitatively and quantitatively .

Made in United States
Troutdale, OR
11/07/2024

24545428R00178